I Try to Behave Myself

PEG BRACKEN'S ETIQUETTE BOOK

DRAWINGS BY HILARY KNIGHT

A FAWCETT CREST BOOK

Fawcett Publications, Inc., Greenwich, Conn.
Member of American Book Publishers Council, Inc.

Dedicated, with love, to Roderick Lull

Acknowledgments are gratefully made to the authors and
publishers who have given their permission to reprint copyrighted
material, as follows: Bergen Evans and Random House, Inc.
for a quotation from the Introduction to Comfortable Words by
Bergen and Cornelia Evans; Romain Gary for material that
appeared in The Ladies' Home Journal and Holiday; Indiana
University Press for lines from Ovid's The Art of Love, translated
by Rolfe Humphries; George Stevens for a quotation from
"George Who?," which appeared in The Atlantic, March 1960;
The Viking Press, Inc. for a quotation from
Ian Fleming's Thunderball.

Library of Congress Catalog Card Number: 64-11534

A dual selection of the Better Homes & Gardens Family
Book Service, March 1965

First Fawcett Crest printing, March 1966

Published by Fawcett World Library,
67 West 44th Street, New York, N. Y. 10036.
Printed in the United States of America.

✔

HOW TO BEHAVE YOURSELF
AND ENJOY IT

In this delightfully irreverent and eminently practical guide, Peg Bracken not only discusses how to plan a wedding, but what happens afterward ("Good Manners and Sex"). She has bright ideas for entertaining, as well as sound advice on how to break the Reciprocal Visit Habit. She tells you how to collect extra men—and how to cope with extra women. She's refreshingly uninhibited on the parent-child relationship ("13 Things Children Should Learn, and the Sooner the Better"). She advises on social lies; on when, how, and whom to tip; on how to interpret a French menu; and provides a wonderfully full and frank list of *in* words to replace such *out* words as "dentures," "little girls' room," and "tummy." In short, she tells you how to behave yourself—and enjoy it.

Foreword

Etiquette is a field that has been well plowed, by more knowledge-able folk than I. When I first set foot on the terrain, I wondered uneasily what I was doing here.

Yet, on examining it more closely, I found it to be a larger field than I had thought, and in poorer shape. I found quicksands which have been widely skirted by even the bravest pioneers, and I found mossy, overgrown areas, as well as some charred stumps which should have been blasted out of there long ago.

Indeed, it has been a journey of discovery for me in many ways, for I have asked many questions and learned many things.

For one, I learned that manners vary greatly depending on your country, time, and tong, as well as your own ideas of what is im-portant. From the crumbling old edifice of formal etiquette, every-one salvages his own bits and pieces. I know a woman who long ago washed those service plates right out of her hair, but wouldn't think of lunching in town without a hat. I know a man who is punctilious about opening car doors for women, but often goes tieless to dinner. More and more, we march to a personal drumbeat.

Then, too, earnest folk—who want to do things correctly—don't always agree. For instance, some say that when you request the honour of someone's presence you must keep the *u* in honour. Others say that h-o-n-o-r is perfectly all right.

And still others say Ho-hum. For the big thing I have learned is that etiquette—which was invented to keep people out—is now dedicated mainly to keeping people comfortable. Once only a proof of your breeding, manners are now an indication of your warm heart and good intentions as well (and if something is temporarily the matter with either, you may as well stay home until the soul's own weather improves).

That is why considerable space is devoted in this book to minor wounds and abrasions: how to avoid them or assuage them.

Then you'll find other practical points: what gentlefolk do, these days (not what some book says they do), about third-person invitations, thank-yous, calling cards, tipping, and so forth—all matters best turned over to automation because it saves headwork.

And there are some items hard to classify. For instance, when a gentleman drinks a champagne toast from your slipper—your evening slipper, that is, not the bedroom type with the pom-poms—you may not properly return the compliment in kind, either from your own slipper or from his English brogue. I am glad to pass this along for the benefit of anyone else who may have been doing it wrong, too.

This, a book about manners, poses a problem in manners: If I were to list all those who have helped me, in one fashion or another, there would have to be a second volume. So I can offer only a general but profound *thank you* to friends near at hand and far away whose generous assistance has been above and beyond the call of duty.

Most especially I would like to express my gratitude to Gay Sandelin, Mary McClintock Bosch, Phoebe Gilkyson, Emily Templeton, Myrza Dickel, Edna Pomon, Geneva Redwine, and Teddy Watson, and to Andrew Anspach, Larry Hilaire, Bill McGraw, Ward Hawkins, and Dr. Lyle Knoder.

I want to express my gratitude, also, to all the people who have explored the area before me and done their fair share of stump clearing.

Among them I am especially indebted to Emily Post. Following John Bunyan's example in the allegorical *Pilgrim's Progress,* she it was who made the use of the symbolic name standard to etiquette writing—a valuable contribution, indeed. When the Toplofties are invited by the Smallenscareds for dinner (and, really, the occasion turned out remarkably well, considering everything), it is helpful to both writer and reader that the situation can be thus implicitly presented.

The device has a certain poetic aptness. For, exploring the region of manners, we all meet up—as Christian did—with Mr. Feeblemind and Mr. Greatheart, with Mrs. Inconsiderate and Mr. Smoothman. We have our doubts, too, and commit our sins, and carry our burdens down the long, crowded thoroughfare.

I will be happy if this book helps someone to travel a little more easily along it, in more comfortable shoes.

—PEG BRACKEN

Upson Downs
Portland, Oregon
August 1, 1963

Contents

NOTE

"... This book ... does not pretend to the wisdom and influence of a teacher. Did I consider myself as in that character, I should hardly venture to put any opinion or even any sentiment into these papers which has not been sanctified by great authority. But as I am only the companion of my readers, I have no scruple to write freely, as they will judge for themselves."

—JAMES BOSWELL
The Hypochondriack, 1777

I

❀

THE
SOCIAL RAMBLE

"The social ramble ain't restful."
—LEROY SATCHEL PAIGE

CHAPTER ONE

Mine Host, Mine Guest, Mine Table Manners

"HOSPITALITY, n. The virtue which induces us to feed and lodge certain persons who are not in need of food and lodging."
—AMBROSE BIERCE

Clearly, it would make for a neater world if everyone read the same etiquette book. Then everyone would be doing the same steps. But not everyone does. Sometimes you are tangoing by yourself. Sometimes you're even off the dance floor, in wild country.

10

Before we wade into this particular jungle, all snake-infested and loud with the cries of strange birds, we must look one fact in the eye: Some people often entertain people they don't want to entertain and who don't especially want to be entertained by them.

Now, sometimes this is because they *must* entertain them—or think they must, which unhappily shoots them into the same dark pocket. But oftener it's lethargy that lets the sad merry-go-round start, and a mistaken sense of duty that keeps it going.

What can happen is this: People sneak up and start something when you're not looking. Invite you to dinner, say. And you go. The evening proves to be one of those little adventures in futility that occasionally beset us all. But, after a bit, you invite *them,* for another of the same. And they invite *you* again. . . .

In truth, both manners and sense dictate that the thing be chopped off clean, right after the first fiasco. It is a nice though unnecessary grace note to send the hostess flowers, with a cordial though noncommittal "Many thanks—it was so nice of you to entertain us!" (Which it was. She wasn't actually to blame for all that incompatibility, any more than you were.) But if you return the invitation, you'll live to regret it, sure as you're born.

Let us remember that everyone's social career, no matter how modest, is littered with bodies. Inasmuch as nearly everyone has been or will be a body at some time or other, to someone else, the situation must simply be understood by all hands, and no hard feelings.

This section will be divided as neatly as possible between the duties and nonduties of the Host and the Guest, but I can tell you right now it won't be as clear-cut as all that. Just as two raindrops plus two raindrops don't necessarily add up to four,* many host-guest matters tend to run into each other.

In many ways, you see, Host and Guest are as interdependent as dancers. Just as the performance suffers when a ballerina *grand jetés* into the arms of somebody who isn't standing there, so can a social occasion suffer—not to mention the Host and the Guest—through lack of mutual understanding.

Consider the guest who drops in. Usually, people who like to drop in like to be dropped in *on,* themselves, and if they would

---

* Sometimes they make a puddle.

only stick to dropping in on each other, there would be no problem. But, being dyed-in-the-fleece dropper-inners, they are seldom at home to be dropped in on.

Therefore, they broaden their field to include the other people—busy people, who might be making whisky in the basement or cookies in the kitchen or love upstairs or are otherwise engaged in any of a hundred fascinating pursuits— in a word, people who hate to be dropped in on but are too polite to say so loudly.

And just consider the stupidity of dropping in on a girl who lives alone in a big city, as well as the stupidity of this same girl should she answer the door—how does *she* know it isn't Jack the Ripper? The police have warned her repeatedly about this.

Well, misunderstandings like this can go on indefinitely, and will, until everyone understands that dropping in—on people whose attitude about it you do not know—has been poor practice since the invention of the telephone.

The same thing holds true of surprise housewarmings, surprise *bon voyage* parties, et cetera. The only difference is that with these affairs you're enabled to show all your friends at once how funny you look in curlers. It is the duty of a good friend to tip off the hostess-to-be, who will of course act beautifully surprised, which is easier for her to do with her teeth in.

". . . Mrs. Golightly only made about two calls a year, and wisely she picked the very days she knew everything would be looking its very best, including Linnea and the children. That made it a pleasure to have her."   —ARDYTH KENNELLY

Then take the generous gardener-guest, who shows up for a dinner engagement bearing an unheralded armload of beautiful blooms. If only she'd phoned the day before to say she was going to, her hostess wouldn't already have used all her containers except the bathtub. Or had to do something with the flowers when she is busy greeting her guests and— Oh, well.

And the volunteer cleanup committee which the protesting hostess is unable to strong-arm out of her kitchen. Here, too, the rule must be stated: If a hostess wants help, she will ask for it. If she doesn't, she won't, and will the ladies please remain seated.

Nowhere, however, are the misunderstandings more plentiful than in the area of punctuality, particularly where the dinner party is concerned.

The fact is, something strange has happened to the simple or informal dinner party. Like a railroad train of six engines pulling one small caboose, it is heavy on the front end. A few decades ago, you ate first, then spent a reasonable while getting acquainted. Now you spend a number of hours getting acquainted and finally eat, if you are staunch enough to last that long.

One trouble is this: When the hostess says 7:00 P.M., she doesn't *mean* 7:00 P.M. She expects some leeway for her last-minute touches. This is a point which most female guests understand, for they are, after all, hostesses occasionally themselves. If they don't, they will get the message shortly, once they've let their husbands talk them into being punctual. Sitting in their host's living room, having admired the cut of his bathrobe as he whisked upstairs to shave, and with ample opportunity to read the bedtime Uncle Wiggily story to the host's children, they feel that this is no Mardi Gras. Indeed, they resolve never to let it happen again.

As a result of these factors (Hostess Factor and Guest Factor), people arrive when they feel like it, depending on their genes, convictions, and baby sitters. And inasmuch as Victor Goodhost presses a drink upon each and every straggler —never let it be said that Victor lets a guest stand around empty-handed—the cocktail hour stretches out, accordionwise, toward 10:00 P.M.

Unfortunately, Victoria Goodhost does little to squeeze it up. Indeed, around 8:30, seeing that her party is going nicely, she decides to join it. In the food department she had planned on something resilient (although few entrees besides cold ham will actually keep their bounce through the long haul from 7:30 to 10:00).* She may go out to the kitchen and turn the oven down, so the casserole can dry out comfortably at 200°. Or, more likely, she'll think the heck with it and stay where she is.

* Although there is a way to handle roast beef through a cocktail time of unpredictable duration, and it is this: At ANY hour of the day from 9:00 A.M. to midafternoon, salt and pepper a six- to eight-pound oven roast—prime rib, rolled sirloin tip, or whatever. You might lard it, too, if you remembered to ask the butcher for extra suet. Then you put it in a preheated 350° oven for one hour. Then

It doesn't much matter, because by the time Victor finally issues the last good ol' dividend from the good ol' shaker, and the guests stroll into the dining room on their hands and knees, they wouldn't know sherried pheasant from a parboiled hot dog.

All this is bad enough. But worse is to come: the dreadful digestive period ahead, when the guests—having said everything, drunk everything, eaten everything—still cannot go home. (*Everyone* learns, as a child, that he mustn't eat and run.) Hence, the impromptu cheerily-'round-the-world-we-go-and-let-the-potato-chips-fall-where-they-may quality of the first half of the evening is equaled only by the unrelieved gloom of the second.

Clearly, ground rules are needed, for both the Host and the Guest. I am happy to be able to provide them here, all pondered upon and passed by a jury of my more knowledgeable peers.

1. The Goodguests will be no more than 20 minutes late to an informal dinner party without telephoning. The exception would be the casual afternoon-into-evening affair—"come around four and see the garden"—which stems from a rough rule of thumb: The earlier the party, the more leeway; the later, the less.

2. The Goodhosts will indicate in their invitations the proposed order of events, and they will mean the time they say. Here, the English system makes superb sense. The invitation reads, "Dinner at the Goodhosts', 7:15 for 8:15." (Or, on the telephone, "Do come at seven fifteen—we're having dinner at eight.") Either way, it means that the 7:55 straggler gets no cocktail—just an "I'm so sorry you weren't here in time for a drink."

And, in truth, 45 minutes to an hour for cocktails is plenty, if there's to be any kind of talk through dinner and after. Go tell it on the mountain.

Let's take a closer look now at

turn off the oven and DO NOT OPEN IT. This is very important. Seal it with freezer tape if your family is nosy. Then, when what you devoutly hope to be the last cocktail is being poured, you trot to the kitchen and turn the oven back on to 350° for exactly half an hour. The roast will be perfectly done if you like it rosy-rare. If you like it more medium rare, leave it 45 minutes instead of 30.

INVITATIONS

The best invitation is the one which best informs the guest of what he's in for. For example, few hostesses invite people for bridge without knowing whether they like it or play it. But many a guest has walked right into a dismal evening of Charades, with no escape. Or Folk Music, or Learning the Bossa Nova (or the *Varsovienne*), or Wine-Tasting, or Home Movies, or just name it—all activities which are fun if you like them and pretty dreadful if you don't. Guests must be forewarned so they may bow out with grace.

What to wear is another problem the hostess should clarify. Most etiquette books don't. They merely explain the difference between Formal Wear (White Tie) and Informal Wear (Black Tie), which butters little parsley in some necks of the woods, where Informal usually means no tie and occasionally no shirt, either.

There is little confusion, of course, among people who move in the same circle or otherwise know each other well. But if Mrs. Goodhost is inviting someone from a different economic or geographical area, she'd better explain. She can say, "Just casual*—sweaters, skirts, whatever's comfortable," or "cocktail dress sort of thing," or whatever she has in mind. (I know a couple who moved from a social circle where a 7:00 P.M.-or-later dinner invitation invariably meant Black Tie, to another where it definitely didn't. They felt like the finest tigers in the jungle, but also a little silly, the first time they went out to dinner in their new locale and were surrounded by nice little afternoon dresses and business suits.)

If Victoria Goodhost doesn't specify what to wear, Shalimar Goodguest may certainly ask her. And if she forgets to ask her, or can't reach her, she'd better get her husband into his dark suit. (These days, most hostesses expect a dark suit unless they specify otherwise.) She herself can then put on a street-length dress with a late-afternoon look, tight enough to show she's a woman and loose enough to show she's a lady. This will take care of most situations.

---

* Casual is a better word than Informal, because its meaning has not been corrupted by the etiquette books.

The Telegraphed Invitation   It is proper, as well as rakish and expensive, to invite people to anything by telegram. But it doesn't make much sense unless your group is madly mobile and you're inviting them for the following night.

The Telephoned Invitation   This, too, is proper. But it is time-consuming, what with busy signals, no one home, and inquiring about the health of the family, because some people will tell you.

Some etiquette books say telephoned invitations should be followed up with written reminders, but I don't see why. Every woman I know answers her telephone with calendar and pencil handy. It is the person-to-person invitation, muttered behind your hand at another social gathering, which had best be confirmed with a written or telephoned reminder. Otherwise, you may find yourself giving a dinner for four instead of the expected dozen, which makes for a lot of leftovers.

The Informal Written Invitation   This is the fastest and easiest. All Victoria does is find her engraved visiting cards,* if she has any, or her informals (see page 86). On them she writes all the important data, above and beneath the engraved name. If something special is happening in the way of entertainment, she writes it in the left-hand corner under the R.S.V.P.

Dinner

7:15 for 8:15, December 14

MR. AND MRS. VICTOR SPLITLEVEL GOODHOST III
   R.s.v.p.
   Tiddlywinks

22 HALIBUT LANE

(Incidentally, she can do all this on plain, unprinted, fold-over note paper, too. In this case, of course, she'd have to write her name as well as the other information.) If Victoria is on a first-name basis with the people she's inviting, she draws a line through the engraved formal name and writes "Vic and Victoria," thus proving that though she possesses these engraved cards or informals, she's still just folks.

---

* And remember to put them in decent-sized envelopes, or the Post Office may not deliver them.

Then, when Shalimar replies, she does so in the same fashion —sends her own little card or informal back, writing on it something like

It will be delightful to see you on December 14.*
Mr. and Mrs. Vladimir Ranchstyle Goodguest

And, assuming that Victoria cozied up to *her* by writing in their informal first names, Shalimar does likewise.

Notice now: Victoria sets the pace and the pattern. (The underlying principle here resembles that of the table-manner rule for spitting things out when you have to: What went in on the fork comes back out on the fork; what went in by the fingers comes out by the fingers.) You answer an invitation in approximately the same fashion it was issued. Although, if you can't stand parlor games like this and can't find any decent note paper around anyway, telephone, for heaven's sake. It's far politer than delaying too long, or not answering at all, which is about as rude as one can be.

(And Shalimar had just better be glad Victoria didn't write the sort of note they're always tossing off in the etiquette books: "Darlings! It's been *light-years* since we've seen you, and we're dying to, so Vic and I've plotted a little dinner party. . . ." To which Shalimar would have had to reply, "Sweeties, what fun! Vlad and I will be enchanted to freeload Saturday night, et cetera. . . ." Actually, those gay little notes read fast, but they write slow.)

"When Dr. Johnson declared that it made things much simpler to know that a lord goes through a door ahead of a commoner, he was no more striking a blow against individualism than against equality: he was only interested in saving everybody time." —LOUIS KRONENBERGER

Here, of course, is the main virtue of the cut-and-dried routine of the engraved third-person invitation: It saves time, by saving headwork, to issue and to answer. (It has other merits as well, for weddings and other solemn occasions; for further discussion, see page 162.) Still, it is something to beware of for purely social occasions other than those extremely ceremonious ones involving royalty or other dignified dignitaries. Otherwise, it tends to make the sender look a little

---

* Or she can regret with "So sorry—we'll be in Hong Kong," or whatever their situation is.

foolish. Millicent Nubile's engagement tea doesn't usually rate that much ceremony, and answering the thing in kind is somehow faintly embarrassing to many people. For Millie's little rites of spring, let's stick to informals.

Regrets Only The use of this, instead of R.S.V.P., is fine if Victoria Goodhost is certain her prospective guests will be in town at the time of her party. But if it's holiday time, or summertime, she'd better not *be* certain. And she'd also better not if it is a large affair she's having catered. The caterer must charge her for the 50 platefuls she ordered, even though 20 people don't show. So it's best to make sure.

One more point about Invitations before we move on: No matter how casual the invitation, Shalimar Goodguest must never assume that her children are invited, unless they specifically were. If for some odd reason she wants to bring them along, or has no one to stay with them, she can explain sorrowfully that she's sitterless. Possibly, then, the hostess may go the second mile and tell her to bring them, they can eat with *her* children, and so forth. Possibly, too, she may not. In any case, the decision is up to the hostess.

Now let's take a closer look at Victoria and her dinner table as she gives the seating arrangement a little thought. Not much. Just a little. After all, it isn't a complicated matter. There's no such thing as sitting below the salt, in this democratic day of individual saltcellars. And, as Bernard Baruch replied, when asked how he seated the notables at his various dinner parties, "I never bother about that. Those who matter don't mind, and those who mind don't matter." This is the sensible approach, unless you land on a terribly tight little island—military, political, diplomatic—in which case there'll be an official Bluebook explaining everything in ghastly detail. Otherwise, Victoria Goodhost may follow the following procedure for her informal dinner, and no one can fault her.

The Guest of Honor She seats the female guest of honor, Mrs. Nobel P. Winner, on the right of her husband, if any, who sits at the other end of the table. (If Mrs. Goodhost hasn't a husband, she can ask a good friend to fill in. If she's *looking* for a husband, this is a good excuse to invite an attractive bachelor or widower or something. She can put it on the basis of his doing her a favor and getting a free meal at the same time.)

She seats the male guest of honor—in this case, Mrs. Winner's husband, probably—on her own right.

If it is an all-female dinner, she seats a good friend at the other end of the table, and Mrs. Winner on her good friend's right.

Then she seats the rest of the guests as she pleases. (It is a wise move, when guests are to sit at small tables, to seat all the bores together. This gets them out of other people's way, and most times they have more fun like this, too.)

At a serve-yourself buffet, if there is a guest of honor, it is a nice touch for Victor or Victoria to escort him or her to the buffet table when the food is ready. If he seems hell-bent on seeing the bottom of the Martini pitcher before he eats, Victoria may correctly bring him a well-filled plate.

The fact is, the guest of honor doesn't always know what is expected of him, or care. Like leaving first (because the other guests shouldn't leave until he does). But I've been to affairs where the G. of H. enjoyed the role so much that he took root. This rule would seem to apply, then, mainly to occasions of ceremony.

The etiquette books, by the way, always make much of this guest-of-honor routine, as though people went around continually honoring other people, which most people don't. Usually, you invite a few couples you like—all created equal and managing to stay that way, more or less—and no one is actually more important than anyone else. What you do in that case is this: If one couple hasn't dined at your house before, turn *them* into the guests of honor. Or if one couple is much older than the rest, let them have it. And if they're all about the same age and equally familiar with your bailiwick, seat at your own right the best-looking man or the one you most enjoy talking to. After all, you've worked pretty hard on this little get-together, and there ought to be something in it for you.

The Extra Woman There are many extra women around these days, and modern etiquette doesn't decree that you must invite a male partner for her (unless this is a severely formal dinner, which we're leaving severely alone). After all, this isn't the mating season, or maybe it is, but she is probably taking care of that department herself. A dinner is a dinner and a date bureau is a date bureau, and the twain don't necessarily have to meet. (This is a good thing to bear in mind in *inviting* an unattached woman, too. It's quite all right to say, "If there's someone you'd like to bring, do bring him," but make it clear that she's just as welcome all by herself.)

At any rate, once the guests are seated, the woman on the right of the host is served first. (The hostess *never* is, unless she's the only woman at the table, or is alone with the family. The purists will frown on her, and she'll never earn her big etiquette E.) Also, the woman-on-the-host's-right's wine is poured first. And her empty plate is removed first. After she is taken care of, it's unimportant what happens next to who or even whom, so long as it happens quickly.

If more than six are at the table, Victoria should suggest that everyone start eating as soon as he is served. And her guests should obey her, with no sash twisting. Otherwise, they'd all be eating lukewarm food, which would be foolish, after all the trouble Victoria took to serve it hot.

Which brings us right into the arena of Table Manners, both practical and puzzling. (Let it not be said that this book leaves a stone unturned, though it's surprising what you find under some of them.)

Practical table manners involve such simple but oft over-looked points as this: The Goodguests must do their level best to eat. After all, Victoria didn't spend all day cooking just for kicks. Her darling is the guest who eats with gusto, not the sick canary, even though the latter may know a *porte-couteau* at 20 paces.

There may, of course, be good reasons why a guest *can't* eat: an allergy, a nervous upset, a diet. If it is an allergy or a limiting diet, it's a good idea to mention the fact when accepting the invitation. If it's a great big allergy or an *extremely* limiting diet, he'd better just decline—perhaps suggesting that he drop in after dinner. Or perhaps Vladimir simply feels like Albert the Airsick Eagle at the sight of a double-cut stuffed pork chop, and can't help it. In any case, he calls no attention to his little problem, but musses the food around somewhat, and throws up a smoke screen of spirited conversation about anything *except* his little problem.

This is where Victoria Goodhost shows the stuff she's made of. She gives no sign of noticing how much or how little anyone eats, and she simply averts her eyes as Vladimir tries to hide his pork chop under his Noodles Romanoff, which he isn't getting too far with, either.

(Come to think of it, Victoria should have concentrated harder on that menu. In this slender-minded day, it's best if the *pièce de résistance* isn't so conspicuously calorie-laden, and she'll be lucky if anyone more than doodles with the noodles.)

Another obligation of the hostess is to provide dental floss in the powder room. This will be appreciated by the guests who did eat the pork chops.

And another obligation of the guest is to say which of two things he prefers, when he is asked. For instance, "Do you want light or dark meat?" It's a poorly equipped turkey that can't provide both, and the host couldn't care less which the guest chooses; he simply wants to get this show on the road.

Then too: The guest should decide quickly whether he wants some of something, then abide by his decision. A distressing habit—generally found, for some reason, among portly elderly ladies—is to say "No, thank you" to the spoon bread or the potatoes, and then, ten seconds later, "Oh, I'll have a *little*."*

Now, no matter what culinary disasters the hostess may have served forth, she must keep her apologies to a minimum. Otherwise, they'll depress her guests even more than the food does. If she snarls that her casserole isn't fit for the dog, they can only insist stoutly that it is, which doesn't help matters. All she can say—if she *must* say something—is a wry "This didn't turn out quite as I'd expected, but no matter." Then she goes gallantly on to other things, remembering you can't win 'em all.

In this connection, it is unwise of Victoria Goodhost to try a new recipe on guests, or to try any faintly out-of-the-way operation she's not wholly sure of. If she serves the Old English Pudding with Flaming Currants, but the currants won't flame, or Cherries Jubilee, and the cherries won't jube, the guests will be very embarrassed, as though they were watching their child flunk a piano recital, and they will wish they were elsewhere.

And so, finally, to a few table technicalities, to which most etiquette books give more attention than they deserve.

"Cleanse not your teeth with the Table Cloth, Napkin, Fork or Knife." ——GEORGE WASHINGTON

* Or a teensy bit. Or a smidgin.

Actually, as the Goodguests know, it is easy to maintain true pitch in the fish-fork department. One simply works from the outside in, trusting the hostess to serve things in their proper sequence. If she doesn't, the whole thing can disintegrate. It is *her* wee disaster, though, not the Goodguests'. But watch out for the oyster fork. If the hostess prides herself on these niceties, it will be found at the FAR RIGHT. Also, she'll expect you to use your individual butter spreader only on your bread. If you want more of the higher-priced spread on your spud, take the butter WITH YOUR FORK from your butter plate. And she may be of the persuasion that places the dessertspoon due north of the dinner plate, parallel with the table edge. So if you're wondering how to eat the blancmange, look up there before you ask.

However, the *raison d'être* of table etiquette is to make the fairly unattractive spectacle of ingesting food as unobjectionable as possible. Whether one uses the right hand or the left hand to raise the fork to the mouth matters little, so long as the mouth remains closed while it chews. (Some people believe you are eating correctly only if the left hand remains in the lap, as you eat with the right. But if you can think of something interesting or constructive to do with the left hand at this time, I can see no reason against doing it.)

As we get down to the fine strokes here, it becomes apparent that there are two easy tests for any table-manner rule.

1. Does it make the business of eating somewhat more aesthetic?

2. Does it serve some practical purpose?

If the answer is Yes to either or both questions, then the rule is probably a good one to observe.

A thoughtful and worldly man of my acquaintance has decided that spooning his soup *away* from him, as the etiquette books decree, makes for sloppier performance, inasmuch as the soup has farther to travel and more chance to drip. He has therefore taken a stand and planted his flag, in a most courageous manner. He spoons his soup toward him, damn the torpedoes, and full speed ahead.

Or you may differ from the authorities on the crumbled-crackers-in-the-soup routine (very bad) and the sopping-up-the-gravy-with-the-bread routine (A-okay if it is a *small* piece of bread powered by the fork, not the fingers). There seems no logic to this distinction, neither operation being a particular joy to watch. Here, it seems to me, it is every man for himself.

If the crackers and the gravy are that important to him, he may as well have at them, so long as he does so with reasonable decorum.

On the other hand, consider the business of placing your knife and fork close together, across the center of the plate, when you've finished eating—the fork on the left, the knife on the right, with its cutting edge facing the fork. At first glance this seems a bit silly. Still, if the tools are in the middle of the plate, they're less apt to fall onto the tablecloth, or onto the floor when the plate is carried away. Furthermore, when the knife's cutting edge is turned inward, there is less chance of cutting the hand that fed you, should it hastily grab the plate to remove it. This, then, would be a good rule to observe, depending on how you feel about your hostess.

(There is good reason, too, for not shaking out your dinner napkin. I know a man who learned this at the home of friends whose serving maid had been trained in the old turn-of-the-century customs. One of these was to wrap a hard roll in each napkin. When he shook out his napkin, the roll ricocheted across the room and nearly broke the window.)

Finger Foods and Nonfinger Foods Here again, reason reigns, or should. If it is a neat, self-contained sort of item that won't smear your fingers—celery, radishes, crisp bacon, potato chips, bananas, et cetera—it's finger food. If it's messy, it is fork food, or knife-and-fork food, that's all.

Admittedly, some things fall into a no man's land: They are messy but still can't be eaten satisfactorily with anything except the fingers—corn on the cob, barbecued spareribs, and so forth. But the kindhearted hostess won't serve these at any except the most informal of informal occasions, so there is really no problem.

When she does serve them, she must also serve individual stacks of paper napkins in addition to the damask, if any. The sensitive female spirit revolts against wiping a well-buttered, catchupped, and lipsticked mouth on a wisp of linen.

All in all, the main thing to beware of at the table is what we might call Intimidated Manners, or manners which are forever taking their cue from somebody else's. They can result in a painful case of tennis-match neck, caused by all those rapid east-west glances up and down the table to see who is doing what with what. Moreover, it can be poor tactics, like cheating in school and copying the wrong kid's paper: You can well end up in worse shape than you'd have been in on your own.

"... *Affected gentility is a mark of being ill at ease. But a deviation from the normal may mean any one of a number of things. Suppose—to illustrate—that a hostess notices one of her guests eating her pie with a spoon. She may think that no fork has been put at the woman's disposal and that, being very polite, she preferred to risk ridicule rather than to call attention to her hostess's oversight. Or the guest may belong to some sect that believes God does not want us to eat pie with a fork. Or she may not know any better. Or she may be a real, flat-heeled aristocrat who eats pie any way she damn well pleases and happens that day to damn well please to eat it with a spoon. But certainly if the guest were in all other ways attractive, intelligent, and poised, the hostess would not be warranted, on the basis of this one peculiarity, in assuming that her guest had no knowledge of the ways of cultivated people."*
—BERGEN EVANS

And now that we've cornered some of the curves of a long social evening with the Goodhosts and the Goodguests, these questions arise: When will they break it up? And how?

Had the Goodhosts entertained at their club or at a restaurant, there'd be no problem. Victoria would sound the curfew —just rise and say, "I think we've about exhausted the possibilities here," or something of the sort—and that's *it*. But at home, the evening can stretch longer than anyone really wants it to. Hosts must be careful here. No matter how beamish they feel, they must quell the urge to insist that the people stay another six hours to hear the new album and finish the brandy —especially if next day is a working day. Instead, Victoria may say, "Of course we'd love to have you stay longer, if you don't have to be up early tomorrow," which at least gives a guest a branch to swing from.

Far more numerous are the dinner guests who don't seem to understand that they weren't invited for overnight. But, even here, there are solutions. Take the guest who calcifies at the open front door. Technically he is leaving, mind you, but he thinks of everything to say except "Good night." You may suggest, "Why don't you come back in and sit down again?" Often this will do it. Or the host and hostess, standing in loose defensive formation, can suddenly put out their hands to shake his, with an "It *has* been nice!" Or the host can say, "I'll go with you to the car," (or the elevator) and lead the way.

Harder is the problem of the guest who won't even get out of his chair, let alone the front door, but says, "We should have left *hours* ago!" and does nothing about it. Some hostesses do well with "Wouldn't you like a cup of hot coffee for the road?"—thus indicating that the bar is closed and the hour is late. (Some, on the other hand, find that this can start things all over again, so one must be careful.) It is perfectly correct, too, for the hostess to rise and say, "I'm so sorry—my husband has a terribly early appointment tomorrow, and I'm afraid we must say good night."

And the host can do his part. I heard of one who—at 2:00 A.M.—announced with mild surprise, "If you people weren't here, I'd have been in bed three hours ago."

Best of all, perhaps, is the solution of a gentle professor I know. When the evening has reached its logical close, he rises and says to his wife, "Come, my dear. Let us go to bed, so that these good people can go home."

CHAPTER TWO

Homes Away from Home

"I feel a slight difficulty in existing. . . ."
—FONTENELLE

It is beginning to look as though we'll never see the last of our little playmates of the western world, the Goodguests and the Goodhosts. But we are still duty bound to tag along behind them through the ups and downs of a weekend visit. Only then can we wave good-by and sail away, letting the sun slowly sink over Hospitality Acres as we head for the nearest motel. (This chapter will touch briefly on hostelries, as well as restaurants, although restaurants will be postponed as long as possible because of all that French.)

Most visits of overnight or longer are arduous work, because it is hard to be nicer than you really are for so long a time. Yet it is necessary to be. The closer people live together, the more important manners become.

Plautus knew all this back in 205 B.C. when he wrote that fish and company stink in three days.* But he might have added that so do hosts, for it's a matter of whose shoes you're standing in. At any rate, the etiquette of a longish visit consists mainly of ways to mitigate a togetherness that would never have happened had both parties only thought the thing through a little sooner.

One good solution or amelioration—for a ménage that is long on children and short on bathrooms,† or just plain short on bathrooms—is to deposit the guests in a nearby hotel, motel, or club, instead of in the back bedroom. This is entirely correct, though more expensive, for the host must, of course, pay the bill. Still, many people feel guilty about it. It is part of the clan tradition to shelter guests under one's own roof. Anyway, one may want to show off one's color TV.

Alphonse et Gaston Much unnecessary bowing and you-firsting is done by some hosts and guests, neither knowing who has or is supposed to have the upper hand. This rule must be clarified: *The host and/or hostess do.* Assuming that they are folk of good will and kindly intentions—which the guests certainly do assume, or they wouldn't have come—they call the shots. After all, it's their life they've invited the guests to share. While they may brisk it up, temporarily, and polish it

---

* This crass-sounding remark is all right to include here because an ancient Roman dramatist made it. If *I* had said it, it wouldn't have sounded so good. This is an interesting though minor point of literary etiquette—just one of the writer's many little problems. One thing, though, it helps guarantee that the writer will give credit where credit is due.

· Speaking of bathrooms, before inviting anyone to your house *any* time, make sure there is a good lock on the bathroom door. Some togetherness-prone families have none, and so do some families with small children who, it is feared, might lock themselves in. But a simple hook arrangement, high up, will avert that little crisis and make visitors more comfortable, too.

a bit, they never aimed to revolutionize it. (A friend of mine—
overnight hostess to an Englishman—was dismayed to find that
he'd left his shoes outside his bedroom door before retiring,
presumably expecting them to be polished. Having no house-
boy, only a husband who patronized the shoeshine stand in
town, my friend very properly sent the Englishman down
there with him the following morning.)

Thus, when Victoria Goodhost turns up the air conditioning
—first asking Shalimar if it doesn't seem awfully warm in
here—Shalimar says, "Yes indeed," and tells her barking
sinuses to pipe down. When Victor Goodhost turns off the
Scarlatti sonata for harpsichord to hear his habitual 11 o'clock
news, Vladimir says, "Hot diggety." In a word, it is up to the
Goodguests to knuckle under, or fit in. This calls for resilience
and the ability to move lightly on the balls of the feet.

Equally, it is the Goodhosts' job to provide something
pleasant to fit into. They must see that there are some good
things to eat and drink, and some reasonably interesting
activities. But it is only fair of them to warn the Goodguests,
before they come, if any of these activities call for special
talents, inclinations, or clothing.

And there'd better not be *too* many planned projects. If the
Goodhosts fill up every golden minute, cruise-director style, the
Goodguests will lose their minds. They must have some free
time, so they can sulk in their rooms and file their nails and
read those good whodunits which the thoughtful hostess un-
failingly stacks in the guestroom.

However, once the program is laid out—once the lasagne
is in the oven and the parcheesi tournament organized—it's up
to the guests to like it.

That's their big job. Then they have some little ones. There's
the matter of *time*. They must inform their hosts, as precisely
as possible, when they'll arrive and whether they'll arrive hungry or well-fed. When a hostess thoughtfully prepares a good
dinner for guests who thoughtfully just had one on the train
to save her trouble, things are off to a lumpy start. Furthermore, they'll announce straight out when they plan to leave.
If Victoria had her wits about her when she invited them, it
was for a specific length of time: "Could you come Friday
evening and stay through noon on Sunday?" or something of
the sort. Even so, the Goodguests must announce promptly
that they're taking the 3:33 on Sunday afternoon.

Trouble and Muss   Now, it's important that the Goodguests pack carefully before they come. Had Shalimar tucked twisted-up tissue paper in the folds of folded things, and left the dry-cleaner's plastic bags on her dresses, she wouldn't have had to latch onto the maid, if any, or the pressing facilities, the minute she hit port. (If she *did* require special services from the maid-if-any, it's to be hoped that she remembered to tip her an extra dollar or so, in addition to the dollar she'd probably leave her anyhow.)

Also, the Goodguests must be neat. They don't make their own beds if there is household help, but if there isn't, they do. They keep things in order, particularly in the bathroom, which might be doubling as powder room for other guests. If Shalimar's complexion comes out of a plastic-lined travel kit, it's all right to leave the kit there, providing it's pretty and discreetly zipped.

Self-Sufficiency   If the Goodguests have any sit-down hobbies or busywork, it's often wise to bring them. No matter what *divertissements* the Goodhosts have planned, it comforts them to know their guests can solo if they have to.

Guests should keep a sharp eye out for points of interest, too. Then, when Victoria says, with a lost look, "I hadn't exactly *planned* anything for this afternoon," Shalimar can leap in with a "Hooray, that'll give me time to explore the cranberry bog" or whatever she noticed on the way in.

Incidentally, if it was an old friend that Shalimar noticed—just imagine, Susie Roommate living right here in Salad Forks, Connecticut!—she'd better not invite her to the Goodhosts' house. This would be about as *faux* a *pas* as possible. But if she mentions the fact of auld acquaintance and hints around, Victoria will probably invite old Susie, herself.

Married daughters sometimes make this mistake when they visit their mothers. Mrs. Youngtype, accustomed now to ruling a roost of her own, forgets that Mrs. Oldtype's roost isn't hers to rule, too. So, when she comes home to visit Mama, she invites people over as casually as she did when she lived there. But if—as is often the case—Mrs. Oldtype likes forewarning and Sèvres and ceremony when she entertains, while her daughter settles happily for spontaneity and sleeping bags, there may be some spirited conversation between them. And Mrs. Youngtype had just better mend her ways, remembering whose house this is.

The Bearing of Gifts   On a first visit to people with children, it's wise to bring the children a gift, for if the children don't like you, they can make your visit pure hell, as they also will if they like you too much. So tread a careful middle ground. Bring the new game or the gay book, but not the $15 baby doll that burps, or the $25 remote-control cosmonaut, life-size.

Then, a few days after returning home, Shalimar may write Victoria a note and send her a small thoughtful gift.* It's easier to choose something now, for now Shalimar knows better what Victoria likes. Or hates. If writing the note proves difficult—because for some reason Shalimar still doesn't feel too comfortable or well-acquainted with Victoria—she can always pretend she is writing the letter to her mother or her best friend. It may get girlish, but that's better than being chilly and awkward.

So much for that. And as for the Goodguests and the Goodhosts, *au revoir* if not good-by. May the sun shine warm upon their faces, and the rains fall soft upon their fields.

HOSTELRIES AND RESTAURANTS

Happily, this section will be short. For one reason, Tipping belongs in the next chapter. For another, most hostelries aren't shy about letting you know exactly the sort of performance they expect. Posted in nearly every hotel room is a clearly printed list of reminders. And the management can throw you out if you don't behave. Indeed, they hold the high cards.

As for other behavior matters, some etiquette books waste whole chapters on away-from-home advice that is instinctively followed, anyway, by anyone who wasn't brought up in a barn. Don't play the radio full blast when other guests might be sleeping. Well, *naturally* not. Don't go barefoot into the roof-top dining room, either. Sometimes you wonder who these books are talking to.

Actually—as I've learned in discussing the matter with hotel-men—there are three important points:

1. *Don't steal things.* When you *want* to steal something—say, a bath towel to complete your collection—ask the manager

---

* For instance, if the food was all right, a copy of *The I Hate to Cook Book,* by Peg Bracken, Harcourt, Brace & World, Inc., 1960.

if you may buy it. Often he'll be happy to sell it to you. Often he'll even give it to you. In any case, you won't feel so funny, then, when you're giving those one-side-of-the-mouth lectures to the children on the virtues of honesty.

A well-known New York hotel once had a run on shower curtains. Mr. Anspach, the manager, was philosophic about it, though wistful. As he said, it was good advertising to have his shower curtains hanging in some of the country's better bathrooms, and had they only asked, they would have received. But their not asking made it hard to maintain the inventory.

2. *Don't spoil things and sneak off*. It often seems easier to move the armchair over the place where you spilled the tomato juice, but it is a coward's trick. The maid or housekeeper won't get mad when you tell her. She'll just be grateful you told her in time, so that she could remove the stain before it became indelibly set.

Plumbing is a particularly sensitive area, and women are always stopping it up. According to a paper-towel manufacturer who, for some reason, has made a study of these things, women will throw anything they can lift into the toilet—pencils, ink bottles, magazines, old hats.

Here again, honesty and forewarning would be appreciated by the hotel or motel management. When a lady has an uncontrollable urge to dispose of her busted umbrella in this fashion, she should let the manager know, so he can rush a plumber to the spot before too much damage is done.

3. *Don't be vague about your comings and goings*. This is more important with hostelries than with a private hostess, for she has no one waiting to rent your room. Thus, it is wise as well as polite to keep the hotel desk thoroughly posted on your schedule changes. Wire or phone if you'll arrive more than an hour late, unless your reservation is securely pinned down with a good fat check. And tell them the minute you decide to stay four days instead of three. Otherwise, though the manager bleeds at every pore as he ejects such an old and valued patron, you may find yourself on the sidewalk with your luggage, watching another old and valued patron move in.

Now to some random restaurant matters before we close in on the *pièce de résistance* of this section, or How to Make Sense out of the Menu.

Restaurant etiquette is indeed a two-way street. Restaurants, both simple and elegant, commit their sins, just as do their patrons.

It would be a great step forward if the counter girl at Nick's, where I stop for an occasional sandwich, would quit swabbing off the catchup bottles with a tired old sponge while I am trying to eat. And *she* probably wishes I'd quit calling her "Miss." After all, one doesn't call the waiter "Mister," and "Waitress" is a perfectly respectable word.

I wish, too, that the waiter at Le Troupeau des Papillons would quit refilling the wineglasses when they are still two-thirds full. It gives me the distinct impression that he wants to hurry us along. (But he, on his part, may be remembering the last time we were there, when we had four cups of coffee and three leisurely cigarettes after dinner without leaving enough tip to cover the time.)

Women and their restaurant peccadilloes are touched upon in Chapter 10. But one point must be stressed: When Marj invites Ernestine to lunch, she must make it crystal clear that she intends to pay for it (if that *is* her intention, Marj and Ernestine not being on a Dutch-treat basis). "May I take you to lunch on Tuesday?" is better than "Will you have lunch with me?" Then, when the waitress presents the check, Marj simply pays, and Ernestine simply lets her, and no argument. If there is a social, time-consuming wrangle, the smiling waitress will want to hit the ladies with a hard roll.

Also, if each is paying her own way, they should ask, as they order, for separate checks. Otherwise, there is the endless business of "Let's see, you had the Beef Pot Pie, that was a dollar thirty, and I had the Tuna Soufflé, that was a dollar ten. . . ." All this, while death and eternity sit glaring.

Men often do these things more neatly. If neither is host, they'll split the check down the middle, no matter who ate what. But Marj and Ernestine will never follow that system, because they are women. It would make them obscurely uncomfortable. All those loose ends and ragged edges.

There is one important thing a man should remember: not to go tieless and sport shirted to a good restaurant, even though it may admit him—which some, unfortunately, will, rather than lose the business. His sloppiness will spoil the candlelit or chandeliered charm of the place for the other customers. Therefore, he is being unkind. Unconventionality should be mainly confined to matters of the mind and conversation, anyhow, for it's more effective that way.

"Natural behavior is not the purpose of civilization. I don't care if you behave naturally or not, but I don't want to see your hairy chest over your sweat shirt when I am eating."
—ROMAIN GARY

MENU FRENCH

"The menu shall be expressed in generally understood plain American terms." —RULE 18, SECTION SIX, The Code of Ethics of the National Restaurant Association

In many an American restaurant, menu French is confusing, not only to guests trying to order, but also to whoever wrote the menu. One can understand the American menu-writer's dilemma. Some Gallic touches are needed, he feels, to make the food sound better. Still, the menu must be understandable, as well as fetching, to guests who don't know French. Too often, therefore, he'll solve his problem by sprinkling the French around like parsley, which results in everything from mild oddities to downright weirdities: *Shrimp Saute' en Wine* (the apostrophe substituting for the accent *aigu* which the typographer didn't have) and *Eggs avec le Black Beurre*, and if you think I am making this up, come see me some time and I will show you around.

Basically, of course, the principle is simple: Classic French dishes have French names that can't be properly translated, any more than "Napoleon" can. It's equally pointless to try to turn a non-French dish into a French one. It is not a *chien chaud*, it is a hot dog.

It is my own feeling (and one is entitled to one's crotchets) that the Cozy Cupboard, where Mom Does the Cooking—and believe me, Mom cooks American—would do better to leave the French alone. Also, a number of good restaurants whose chefs truly know and practice their *haute cuisine* would do well to hire a knowledgeable gourmet to edit their menus.

As the old phrase has it, whatever you are, be a good one.

Now let us consider the problem of the customer who knows no French and is faced with a purely French menu in a good French restaurant (which isn't an uncommon situation, this science-oriented day, with college French being so often bypassed for Nuclear Physics 101). He cannot, alas, always trust the waiter. The waiter may tell him that the Something Argenteuil is especially fine, which may mean that it is or that the chef has prepared quite a lot of it. (Even the best chefs occasionally miscalculate.) In any case, if our friend is allergic to asparagus, he is going to be sorry when the dish shows up, as he will be, too, if the operative word is Florentine and he doesn't like spinach.

Hence, this abbreviated list of some frequently encountered French menu terms. It is offered in the diffident hope that people who have forgotten *la plume de ma tante* or never heard of it may find some of the words helpful.

GLOSSARY

(NOTE: The more transparent French words have been omitted. After all, it isn't hard to equate *truite* with trout or *saumon* with salmon, once you're sure you're in the Fish Department: *Poissons*. Also, *le, la, à la,* and so forth have been omitted in most cases for the sake of brevity. Pronunciation isn't important. You can point to the *escargots* as you order the snails.)

HORS D'OEUVRES

crêpe farcie: a small pancake, stuffed, though heaven knows with what. Crêpes creep about on French menus, and you'll find them in other places than Dessert.

escargots: snails, usually cooked in their shells with a lot of butter and garlic

jambon fumé: smoked ham

(*saumon fumé*, smoked salmon)

pâté: finely mashed meat (usually including some liver) packed with spices and wine

rillettes: minced pork, served, as a *terrine* is, from a little pot. Spread it on crackers if you feel like it.

POTAGES: Soups

crème à l'oseille: cream of sorrel soup

du Barry: cauliflower

orge: barley

petite marmite: reasonably

hearty beef and vegetable soup served in individual casseroles

Vichyssoise: cold potato soup flavored with leeks

OEUFS: Eggs

POISSONS: Fish

coquilles St. Jacques: scallops.
Coquille also means shell. *La
coquille de homard,* lobster
served in the shell. (Don't
confuse this with *en cocotte,*
which means in a casserole.)

écrevisses: crayfish
grenouilles: frogs' legs
homard: lobster
huîtres: oysters
moules: mussels

VOLAILLES: Fowl

caneton: duckling
canard: duck
pigeonneau: squab; often prepared *à la crapaudine*—cut

open and broiled
poussin: tender young chicken
poulet: chicken

And if you see the word *suprême* after some sort of fowl,
it means the entire uncut large muscle stripped from the
breast of a bird. It's used loosely, though. I know a chef whose
pride and joy is Crab *Suprême*—crabmeat in puddles of
butter, served in little shells. Very good, too.

GIBIER: Game

caille: quail
chevreuil: venison
lièvre: hare; *civet de lièvre* is

jugged hare
lapin: rabbit
perdreau: partridge

Another thing: When you see *salmi,* or *salmis,* that's a stew
or ragout of roast game, often served on toast.

VIANDES: Meat (*usually found under* Entrées—*main dishes*—
and Grillades—*grilled meats*)

agneau: lamb
boeuf: beef
jambon: ham
veau: veal; *escalope de veau* is

a collop or piece of veal
ris de veau: sweetbreads
rognons: kidneys

If you want steak of some sort:

châteaubriand: cut from the
thickest part of the tenderloin
—generally considered the
most succulent and tender
entrecôte: a rib steak, cut fair-

ly thick and usually browned
tournedos: the beef that lies at
the narrow end of the tenderloin of beef; usually just
quickly sautéed and garnished

Then, sometimes it's reassuring to know just which part of the animal you're going to be faced with. Like this:

carré de: breast of
côté de: side of
cuisse de: leg of

râble de: back of
selle de: saddle of
tranche de: slice of

LEGUMES: Vegetables

aubergine: eggplant
cèpes, champignons, girolles,
or *morilles:* mushrooms
chou: cabbage

chou-fleur: cauliflower
épinards: spinach
haricots verts: green beans
laitues: lettuce

FRUITS: Fruits

anana: pineapple
cerises: cherries
fraises: strawberries

framboises: raspberries
poire: pear

DESSERTS

cerises jubilées: cherries, brandied and flaming
pêches jubilées: peaches ditto
gâteau: cake
marrons glacés: chestnuts in syrup

profiterole: cream-filled pastry puffs
sabayon: wine-custard pudding or sauce

Now to some miscellaneous terms. First, a number of disappointments—terms for dishes or garnishes which don't turn out to be quite as exciting as they looked on the menu.

Alexandre: just means red and green. This could be dyed pineapple or beets-and-beans or Christmas jello.
anglais: boiled or roasted, usually boiled
bonne femme: simple hearty food cooked as a housewife would cook it
Clamart: with green peas, can you beat it?
Croissy or crècy: flavored

with turnips or carrots
dauphin: with egg sauce. In fact, anything like *dauphine* —*dauphinois* or *dauphinée*— you may suspect of being eggy.
demi-deuil: technically, "half mourning." Means garnished with black and white.
fermier: farmer style: hence, garnished with carrots, cauliflower, lettuce, potatoes

flamand: doesn't mean flaming, but Flemish; often flavored with beer, or vinegar and served with cabbage

florentin: with spinach

irlandais: Irish; hence, with boiled potatoes

limousin: with sausage meat or sausages

lyonnais: with onions

Mayerbeer: with kidneys

mongole: sauce of puréed peas, beans, and tomatoes

Niçois: with tomatoes, often with herbs, olives, and peppers, too

parmentier: just means with potatoes; named for M. Parmentier, a gourmet who loved them

printanier: with several spring vegetables

provençal: tomatoes, olive oil, and a lot of garlic

And, finally, to some items which are luxurious or interesting or otherwise worth the trouble:

amirale: garnished with sliced lobster and fried oysters

Bagration: à la Bagration means "cooked in the finest possible manner." (Refers to the Russian Count Bagration, an employer of Chef Marie-Antoine Carême, who is considered by many to be the father of modern cooking.)

bigarade: seasoned with the rind and juice of a sour orange; often with duck or duckling

cévenale: with chestnuts

financier: prepared as only the rich can afford; hence, with larks' tongues, Napoleon brandy, et cetera, et cetera

maréchale: covered with chopped truffles before being sautéed

normande: with apples, cider, or applejack

périgueux: with truffles

piémontaise: with *white* truffles!

Richelieu: garnished with artichoke bottoms, truffles, asparagus tips

St. Hubert: with venison (St. Hubert is the patron saint of huntsmen)

French restaurants have many ways of telling you that this is something they thought up, themselves. For instance, they'll say: *Rognons d'agneau maison,* which means lamb kidneys the way we do them here. Or, *Rognons d'agneau à notre manière.* Same thing. Or, *Rognons d'agneau chez nous.* Ditto. Or. *Rognons d'agneau Henri,* lamb kidneys the way Henri does them, or did them, for Henri may be dead and gone. On the other hand, he may be the present chef, alive and cooking in the kitchen. In either case, it is perfectly correct to ask the waiter just *how* Henri does them, or did them. There's no point in keeping things like this a secret. You don't want the recipe, for heaven's sake. You just want to make sure you won't run into too much fennel or saffron or something.

One thing to observe, however, is this: When you see something on the menu like *Le suprême de sole maître d'hôtel*, it doesn't mean that this is the hotel's specialty, or the restaurant's. Maître d'hôtel is the name of a simple butter-parsley-and-lemon-juice sauce which many an honest housewife has been using for years, never knowing it had a name.

Now, all this isn't to say that some all-American menus don't need translating, too. To illustrate, your Lumberjack's Rasher of Country-sliced Bacon from Happy Corn-fed Iowa Hogs, Hickory-smoked for That Real Old-fashioned Back-Home-on-the-Farm Flavor, Broiled to a Crisp Delectable Turn means a slice of fried bacon.

But a complete glossary of these terms would take another even longer chapter, and luckily we haven't room.

CHAPTER THREE

The Genial Vices

"One last word and warning," said the Duke. "I would not trust the Golux overfar. He cannot tell what can be from what can't. He seldom knows what should be from what is."

—JAMES THURBER

Now, most etiquette books seem to contain more gravy than meatballs. They tend to shut their eyes to life as it is lived. But not every boat you get into is the good ship Lollipop. Not

every story has a jolly ending, or every situation a perfect
solution.

Bearing these things in mind, then, let us consider the
existing cold war between the smoker and the nonsmoker.

" *'Please smoke,' she said in a magnanimous yet crushed
voice. . . .*"   —LEO TOLSTOY

Smokers and nonsmokers will never see eye to eye. The nonsmoker can't comprehend that good raw clutch at the bron-
chials and the resultant feeling of dim placidity which the
smoker feels with his first drag on a fresh cigarette. The
smoker can't understand what the nonsmoker does with his
time. The best the two can hope for is an armed truce.

In all fairness it must be admitted that smokers annoy nonsmokers more seriously and more often than the other way
around. I know of no smoker who ever got sick from watching
a nonsmoker not smoking. But I do know some people who
turn pea green at one sniff of the smoke from a cigarette or
a pipe or a cigar.

Furthermore, the smoker's sins against etiquette outnumber
the nonsmoker's five to one. Still, the nonsmoker can usually
comfort himself, as he digs the butts out of the dirt around
his philodendron, by reflecting on the latest lung-disease
statistics. And the smoker can always assuage his hurt feelings
—caused by that lady's icy stare on the bus—by lighting
another cigarette.

Let's remember, too, that, smokers annoy *other* smokers.
One complicating factor is the international butting order:
The pipe smoker looks down at the cigarette smoker, and they
both look down upon the cigar smoker.

So let us consider the basic rules each group should abide
by, in order to live in moderate comfort together.

Good Manners for the Nonsmoker   He really ought to provide some decent ash trays* in his quarters, at least one ash
tray per room. This will cut down the number of butts in the
potted plants. And if he will keep some sand-filled flowerpots
outdoors, on the patio or the lawn, smokers won't be so apt

---

* Smaller than a breadbox, bigger than a tangerine, and grooved
for the specific purposes of keeping cigarettes from a) burning
themselves out and b) slipping off onto the table top. No porcelain
pin trays; no lalique shells.

to grind out their cigarettes on the tile or flip them onto the grass to ugly themselves away.

He shouldn't expect to be asked, by a cigarette smoker, if he objects to smoking, unless he is over 90 or unless this ill-matched pair should find itself in a small closed compartment, like a telephone booth. Asking permission is expected today only of pipe and cigar smokers.

He mustn't whisk an ash tray away the minute it holds an ash, for the smoker doesn't really notice these things until his ash tray runneth over. The big danger here is that the non-smoker will whisk away an ash tray holding the true shank of the smoke: a cigarette which has burned down to its—for the smoker—precisely perfect length and feeling of lived-with comfort. (With some smokers this is 1⅝ inches, with others, 1½ inches.)

And the nonsmoker must use a pleasant Approach Direct, instead of a pained look, when the wind wafts smoke in his face. He must *ask* the smoker please to move his cigarette or the ash tray. (Smokers are often absent-minded and unper-ceptive, although they don't mean to annoy people. But pained looks annoy *them*, and they tend to answer with a good puff.)

Good Manners for the Smoker He mustn't smoke in eleva-tors. Cigarette smokers are especially prone to palm their cigarettes for the short ride down to 5, which is against most building regulations and burns holes in people's clothes.

He mustn't smoke where there are NO SMOKING signs, for these usually mean business. It is bad form to explode a plane-load of people or blow a hospital sky-high. He must use whatever self-control he can scrape together on long bus rides, especially in bad weather when the windows are closed.

He mustn't go smoking to the table when he is a dinner guest in someone's house. Perhaps it holds no ash trays; the hostess may have planned to set them forth later. If she does not, by the end of the meal, the smoker may correctly ask for one. Using his saucer or plate is Pigsville. (So is dropping a cigarette butt into a toilet without flushing it promptly.)

Pipe smokers have long been considered the nobility of the smoking fraternity, for reasons that are not immediately clear, and the longer you think about them, the fuzzier they become. The pipe smoker's ash tray, full of decayed yellow pipe clean-ers garnished with dottle, is actually pretty disgusting, no matter how virile the pipe smoker may look biting his briar. Pipe smokers should clean up after themselves, and quickly.

Also, remembering that some people dislike pipes just on general principles, from the pipe smoke itself to the sucking noises pipe smokers so often make while playing with their pipes, the pipe smoker should, in most indoor situations, ask permission. Then, when he gets it, he should pay particular attention to audience reaction. The all-pervasive aroma of some of the sweet rum-fudge-and-butterscotch mixtures would gag a goat.

Cigar smokers must always ask permission anywhere. And they mustn't leave those big, fat, chewed, soggy cigar butts in ash trays. They can bury them or flush them or swallow them—no matter, but they must do something.

The cigar smoker must be careful, too, about invading feminine quarters with stogie in hand. A cigar-smoking man, picking up his wife at the hairdresser's, can quickly have the shop smelling like the City Hall. This is unkind both to the ladies and to Mr. Tony.

Women Who Smoke Etiquette rules for the woman smoker are the same as those for men, except for the fact that she can't smoke on the street and look ladylike. Even today, this gives her a Sadie Thompson or beatnik or washerwoman effect, depending on her age and build.

Two errors in etiquette are still committed occasionally by the woman smoker. One is never having cigarettes or matches, only the habit. Most men consider this fairly charmless. (And these lassies learn quickly, of course, that they can't get away with it at all, with other women.) The second error is expecting her cigarettes to be lit for her, even though matches are on the table beside her. I know a camellia blossom who will sit end-lessly with cigarette poised, waiting for some man to quit whatever he's doing and light it. This is bad manners, for it makes other people uncomfortable, and it is not the action of a lady, but of a blob of glup.

Which brings up the question: When *should* a man light a woman's cigarette? Most women would answer, *not* when he must cross the room to do so. If a man lunges with a lighter from 15 feet away every time she fumbles, a woman will presently get the uneasy feeling that she's smoking too much. And he shouldn't butt in if she has her own cigarette lighter all ready to flick.* After all, she didn't bring that cute little gadget along for a paperweight. She likes to use it and show off its pretty monogram. Also, lighting her own cigarette gives her a small feeling of accomplishment, which, in this push-button age, isn't to be sneezed at.

One more tobacco crumb: Formerly, when two smokers were lighting up, it was *de rigueur* to light one's own cigarette first. But that was in the days of sulphur matches, when the first cigarette lit was apt to taste of the fumes of hell. Today, courtesy dictates that the lighter light his own last.

DRINKING MANNERS

"Drinking is in reality an occupation which employs a considerable proportion of the time of many people; and to conduct it in the most rational and agreeable manner is one of the great arts of living." —JAMES BOSWELL

Some people think that showing a pretty reluctance about having another drink makes finally having it more virtuous. But this isn't so. It merely takes some of the fizz out of the soda, while a little enthusiasm puts some in. As our itinerant yardman says, when asked if he'd like another for the road, "I'm your huckleberry!"

Another thing: In definitely *refusing* a drink at any time, you needn't say, "No, thanks, I don't drink"—after all, no one asked you that, exactly—or "It's too early in the day for me." This one may have the drink profferer thinking nervously that it's probably too early for him, too, but he won't like you for bringing the subject up. A simple "No, thanks" is always sufficient.

In this matter of proffering drinks, it is wise of Victor Goodhost to ask not a general "What'll you have?" but a specific "Would you like Scotch? Bourbon? Rye? Sherry? A Martini?"

In reply, Shalimar Goodguest doesn't say she'd like a Chelsea Sidecar. And she doesn't say, "Oh, whatever you're drinking," or "Whatever's the least trouble." Shalimar mustn't

---

* Although if she is using an unobtrusive matchbook imprinted HYMIE'S GAS STATION, he might as well.

shilly-shally, she must *choose*. She is a big girl now and must take it for granted that her host stands ready, able, and willing to prepare whatever he listed.*

Another point of etiquette Victor Goodhost might observe— a point especially important to his female guests—is this: He can let them know if he is using an outsize jigger, particularly if the drink is a strong-flavored one which hides the taste of the liquor. A Bloody Mary that's half vodka and half tomato juice will torpedo the unsuspecting customer, which isn't fair.

Also, he can jolly well quit refilling half-empty cocktail glasses. *The time to refill a cocktail glass is when it is empty.* Then Shalimar has some idea of how merry she is becoming. Some women, it is true, have their own personal gauges. A friend of mine says that on the first drink she sees clearly how witty her friends are. On the second, she realizes how witty she is, herself. On the third, when she knows she is beautiful, too, she knows it is time to eat. But not everyone is so clear-sighted.

As you may have noticed, we seem to be in the middle of a cocktail party, where we may as well stay for a bit in order to touch on some of its more liquid aspects. (Although, should other aspects arise, we'll have to do something about them, for there's no telling when we'll pass this way again.)

Cocktail parties have been greatly maligned, usually by people who keep going to them. The fact is, the cocktail party has much in its favor. Going to one is a good way of indicating that you're still alive and about, if such is the case, and that you're glad other people are, without having to spend an entire evening proving it.

Whether it is the Cocktail Party Proper (with wee napkins and canapés) or the Cocktail Party Improper (with old Chuck tuning his zither for a fast go at "Who Put the Aphrodisiac in Mrs. Murphy's Applejack?"), the problems involved are much the same.

Ground Rules for Hosts   Let's take first things first. It is an important point of etiquette for Victoria Goodhost to make

---

* Once I knew a girl who would wrinkle her pretty nose, when asked if she wanted a Manhattan, and say, "Let's see, is that the one with the olive or the cherry?" But this never went over too well.

crystal clear, in her invitation, the extent of her intended largess. If this is to be a low-budget show, with whisky and peanuts (as many good cocktail parties are), her guests are forewarned and can proceed with their own personal dinner plans.

This is especially important in inviting people who'll have to hire baby sitters or who live at a distance. Mrs. Goodhost must make it immediately clear that there'll be no dinner, for most people aren't thirsty enough to go to all that trouble for a drink. They can then regret, swiftly and gracefully, with a Social Lie (see page 65).

But if she plans to serve elaborate food, it's only fair to come straight out and call it a Cocktail Buffet. Otherwise, her female guests will be miffed. They'll think, "Shucks, this is enough for dinner, only there's that darned ham in the oven and the folks coming over." Also, should Victoria underplay her little party in this fashion, she'll have made a tactical error, for a cocktail buffet usually rates a return dinner invitation, but plain cocktails don't.

Now if the Goodhosts are giving a small party—say seven or eight people—good manners don't necessitate the fancy footwork one often sees as host and hostess strive never to be out of the room simultaneously. Guests can always find something to talk about, even though it's only to criticize the wallpaper. Also, too much attention to this foolish detail has the guests thinking you're afraid they'll steal the silver.

If it is a *large* cocktail party, the Goodhosts needn't introduce everyone to everyone, either. In this situation, the roof is the introduction. After a guest has been introduced to one or two people, he makes his own way, which he'd much rather do, of course, than meet 30 strangers all at once. Besides, the hostess who continually breaks into conversational groups to introduce someone they'd eventually meet anyway is a true disaster.

This isn't to say that the Goodhosts shouldn't keep an ear cocked to all the talk, when they can. Should it head for channels uncomfortable to someone, it is their business to steer it around the reefs. A friend of mine is talented at this. One evening at her house a guest mentioned a dago (or perhaps it was a wop or a hunky). "Now, let's see," she said, with bright, big-eyed innocence. "Just which nationality is *that*? I always get those names mixed up." And if subtlety doesn't work, bluntness will. Victoria Goodhost can say, clearly, "I prefer that we change the subject." As captain, she can run a taut ship if she likes.

She can even—properly—toss people overboard. One of my friends was standing beside her hostess at a large cocktail buffet when a shy young Chinese medical student came up to speak to her. While the three were chatting, a jovial tosspot named Jones joined them, embraced the hostess and boomed in the general direction of the medical student, "You Chinee?" The hostess immediately called one of the caterer's men. "Mr. Jones is just leaving," she said. "Will you help him find his coat and see that he gets in his car?" Mr. Jones seemed puzzled, but he left meekly.

Just a few more points for the host, here, before we come to the cocktail-party guest, who has his little problems, too.

How to Keep from Running Out of Liquor, Which Is Very Poor Etiquette, Indeed   You buy a good deal more of it than you think you'll need. Basically, figure three two-ounce drinks per customer. This means that one bottle (⅘ of a quart) will take care of almost five people. Then get another bottle of each type of liquor you're serving, for insurance purposes.

How to Keep from Running Out of Ice   If you forgot to get big cellophane bags full and freeze them, and if you're short on ice-cube trays and neighbors, you can use plastic egg trays. They make pretty, half-spherical ice cubes, and a half-spherical cube is an interesting thing in itself. But, actually, who has a lot of plastic egg trays? The best thing to do is just freeze water in an aluminum cake pan and chip it with an ice pick.

What to Do if Your Husband Is a Poor Bartender, or if You Live Alone and Would Rather Join the Party than Tend Bar, but You Don't Want to Hire a Bartender   You ask one of the guests, in advance, if he will officiate. Or you serve a cocktail punch rather than individual drinks. For a punchbowl you can use any big salad bowl or pot that you happen to have. Or, logically enough, you can use a punchbowl, bought, rented, or borrowed. A good punch to make in it—not a knockout punch, but a punch which leaves people feeling merry rather than slugged—is this classic:

FISH HOUSE PUNCH

1 quart brandy
1 pint peach brandy
1 pint rum (light)
2 six-ounce cans frozen lemon juice
1 cup light corn syrup, then taste it. Add ½ cup more if you like.
2 quarts plain sparkling water

Mix all the ingredients except the sparkling water, and let them get acquainted for at least an hour. Then pour it all over a block of ice, or a flock of ice cubes, in your punch bowl. Add the sparkling water just before you serve it. This makes approximately 142 ounces of drinking material, which isn't as lavish as it sounds because 76 ounces of it is noninebriating. Therefore, this serves about eight people adequately, and if you've invited more people than that, you'd better double it.

What to Do if Someone Gets Slugged Anyway*   Actually, the Goodhosts should have foreseen this. After all, they've known Chuck for a long time. Unfortunately, though, the traits that get you into a situation usually prevent your solving it. The Goodhosts' warm hearts were responsible for including Chuck in the first place, and now these same warm hearts keep them from calling the cops.

The wisest thing Victoria Goodhost can do is make sure she has some thick soup keeping hot and hidden in the double boiler. She feeds it to him, with plenty of crackers. Any canned chowder or *minestrone* will do. This isn't *haute cuisine,* remember, it's just hot soup. After Chuck has had a couple of bowlfuls, she can then call a cab, and he can pick up his car the next day. If the soup doesn't do it, he'll have to clutter up the guest room or the shakedown bed. But the Goodhosts owe it to society not to turn him loose on the freeway.

. . .

* I know a host who controls, with fair success, his guests' alcoholic intake. Before a gathering, he mixes three big jars each of Martinis and Manhattans, in diminishing strengths (the Number 3 jug containing as much water as alcohol). And he serves three drinks, one from each. This conserves both his cash and the health of his guests, his motives being about half-and-half, like Jug 3.

Finally, as we saw in Chapter 1, there is always the matter of getting people to go home. At a cocktail party, guests should observe, or make a pass at observing (see page 14), the clearly stated curfew. If they don't, and the host and hostess have other plans or are simply tired, there is only one course open: They put on their own coats and hats at 7:30 (if the cocktail hour was announced as 5:00 to 7:00 P.M.) and circulate among the guests looking harried and helpless. "We'd *no* idea it was so late," Victoria murmurs. "Do let me help you find your coat." Then hosts and guests leave together, with the hosts taking a short ride or a walk around the block.

Ground Rules for Guests   Now for a brisk look at the points which Shalimar and Vladimir Goodguest should remember. (Cocktail-party guest imperatives are comparatively few, which is one reason people like cocktail parties. The guest's lot, as well as the host's, grows steadily more miserable; see Chapter 2.)

They needn't arrive on time, of course. No one ever came to a 5:00 to 8:00 P.M. cocktail affair at 5:00 except the cateress (and she should have arrived at 3:30). The larger the party, the wider the margin. The Goodguests may arrive at 7:45, if they like, though at that time they're apt to find the canapé plates stripped to the celery. However, they must *leave* at 8:00, or at least make the proper motions. The Goodhosts can then urge them to stay or not, as they see fit. (Had Victoria given this party preceding another affair—say a community dinner or an art museum showing—everyone would have a deadline, a most satisfactory state of affairs. Many hostesses entertain in this fashion for just that reason.)

Now, the Goodguests mustn't mention that they've just come from the Richenfatts' party, or are Going On to the Hooplahs'. It makes a hostess feel sandwiched in, not to mention forlorn and jealous, to think of someone going on to brighter pastures while she baby-sits that toppling tower of dirty glasses. (Just as, of course, one shouldn't mention any party, past or future, in front of people who weren't invited, unless the party was ten years ago or 2,000 miles away. Even though there's no earthly reason they *should* have been invited, they may feel faintly wounded. Many a mother drills this fact into her children, then forgets it herself, rehashing last night's blast with Mrs. A., who was there, in front of Mrs. B., who wasn't.

One's social life is best left a secret between oneself and one's hairdresser.)

Another thing: Shalimar and Vladimir can remember not to shake hands, at cocktail parties, unless the person to whom they're being introduced puts his hand out first. In this case, they must, but it's a shame. The hand that holds the highball is a damp and clammy mitt. Also, a woman, when a hand is proffered, must do a difficult juggling bit with purse, gloves,* drink, and shrimp-on-a-toast-square, and it simply isn't worth it.

Most important of all, in order to be *truly* Goodguests, prepared for any contingency, Shalimar and Vladimir must make sure that their Personal Liability Insurance policy is paid up and all in order. A payment of $12.50 annually allows them to do up to $10,000 worth of damage to someone else's property, which would admittedly be quite a party.

But just think of the superb manners Vladimir can show, the next time he burns a hole in the middle section of somebody's sofa! Instead of hiding it with a cushion, he can apologize profusely to Mrs. Goodhost and give her the name of his insurance company. And when Shalimar spills her Drambuie on the off-white carpet, and her hostess—biting her lip— bravely protests that it doesn't matter a *bit*, Shalimar can say, "Oh, but it does!" Then the Goodguests—courtesy of their friendly insurance company—can do the handsome thing.

Certainly, the Goodguests should be more careful than these incidents would indicate. But accidents can and do happen, and friendships as well as furnishings stay in better repair when an insurance company is standing behind any chaos you may leave in your wake.

Many people wonder what to do with the fruit in the old-fashioned. What you do with it is eat it, for it's all been marinated in the whisky, including the orange rind, which will stave off scurvy. Then you deftly place the naked toothpick in the ash tray. (If you don't like it, ask for a simple whisky and bitters, next time around, and avoid the whole problem.) If the drink is a tall collins or punch, and the fruit isn't impaled

---

* For she is, of course, gloveless when she eats, drinks, or smokes. Sometimes, to be sure, a girl will keep her gloves on for these activities (*if she doesn't, who'll know she wore any, for heaven's sake, and anyway they're real French suede*), but it has other people wondering which hay wagon she rode into town.

on a toothpick, fishing it out can be messy. In this instance, you use the muddler to smash the fruit against the inside of the glass, thus releasing its delicious natural flavors. If you want to eat it, though, and if a long spoon has been thoughtfully provided, you certainly may.

As for what to do with the pits in the olives—besides letting them pile up into revolting little mounds in the ash trays—there is no problem, for Victoria Goodhost serves only the pitted kind.

On Bringing Your Own Liquor to Someone Else's House
This is a touchy subject, for attitudes vary with people and circles and situations and friendships and places. Some hosts are insulted at the thought. Others start to brighten the minute they see that long brown paper bag coming up the walk. One must know one's host.

In general, this can be said: If it is in any way a formal cocktail party, you don't. If you drink more than makes sense, and visit more often than you are visited, it is good public relations to bring along an occasional gift of good liquor. With a ribbon around it. Ditto when you stop to see people and coincidentally use their swimming pool. Also: In visiting old friends who are so unlucky as to live in one of our country's historic or vacation meccas, you'll probably find your bottle welcome as the flowers in May. Once the word leaks out in the *Alumni Bulletin* that Bud and Bernie have settled in Las Vegas or Williamsburg or Honolulu, it's Nellie bar the door to that steady stream of old college chums unless they come equipped.

One other thing about drinking hard liquor before we get into not drinking hard liquor: Perfectionists in these matters find it aesthetically unpleasing to see someone mix good liquor with sweet soda. But if you like it that way you might as well drink it that way, and they can shut their eyes. (Some coffee connoisseurs consider it sinful to add whisky or brandy to coffee, for a Coffee Royale. Boston Clam Chowder people can't forgive Manhattan Clam Chowder people for living, and vice versa, and so it goes.)

On Not Drinking Hard Liquor
 "Papa says if you don't watch it people will force you one way or the other, into doing what they think you should do, or into just being mule-stubborn and doing the opposite out of spite." —KEN KESEY

Arm twisting is always bad form. If someone says No, he doesn't want a drink, it is best to leave it at that. Maybe he just got rid of a big monkey on his back. Or maybe he has a small one which he doesn't want to grow up. Or maybe he had six drinks before he came. In any case, it is, of course, his own business.

And it must be remembered that there is nothing the matter with not drinking. Some perfectly nice people don't.

The Secret Nondrinker Iced tea is a good thing to keep handy for the person who doesn't drink but doesn't want to advertise the fact. So is ginger beer, which has a stouter taste than ginger ale, though that is good, too. Some ginger beers look like pale whisky and soda, and some are practically colorless. So is bitter lemon, which looks like a Tom Collins.

Then there is the SCHOOLMARM'S KISS: strong bouillon, with ice, in a highball glass.

And the WYATT EARP: half-and-half orange and pineapple juice poured over ice cubes in an old-fashioned glass.

And the BLOODLESS MARY: Add a dash of Worcestershire and a good dash of Tabasco to tomato juice, and pour it over the ice cubes in an old-fashioned or highball glass.

Then, should gin or vodka be the order of the day, in tall drinks, a nonalcoholic lemonade blends nicely with the background. You can make a good inexpensive one like this:

NONALCOHOLIC LEMONADE MIX

Squeeze the juice from 8 lemons and mix it with a big can of grapefruit juice and a pound of sugar. Keep it in a big jar in the refrigerator, and when you serve it, just put a tablespoonful into a glass with ice in it, and fill it up with water.*

* This is better with gin in it.

CHAPTER FOUR

The Highwaymen
Come Riding, Riding: The Tip

"... *The martinis arrived. Leiter took one look at them and told the waiter to send over the bar man. When the bar man came, looking resentful, Leiter said, 'My friend, I asked for a martini, not a soused olive.'*

"*He picked the olive out of the glass with the cocktail stick. The glass, that had been three-quarters full, was now half full.*

"*Leiter said mildly, 'This was being done to me while the only drink you knew was milk. I'd learned the basic economies of your business by the time you'd graduated to Coca-Cola. One bottle of Gordon's gin contains sixteen true measures—double measures, that is, the only ones I drink. Cut the gin with three ounces of water and that makes it up to twenty-two. Have a jigger glass with a big*

*steal in the bottom and a bottle of those fat olives and you've got
around twenty-eight measures. Bottle of gin here costs only two
dollars retail, let's say around a dollar-sixty wholesale. You charge
eighty cents for a martini, a dollar-sixty for two. Same price as a
whole bottle of gin. And with your twenty-eight measures to the
bottle, you've still got around twenty-six left. That's a clear profit
on one bottle of gin of around twenty-one dollars. Give you a dollar
for the olives and the drop of vermouth and you've still got twenty
dollars in your pocket. Now, my friend, that's too much profit. . . .'"*

—IAN FLEMING

Felix Leiter, the speaker, was an admirable secret agent, and I
couldn't have been sorrier when he was eaten up by the
sharks. But he made a surprising omission here: the tip. Forty
cents would be the probable tip for a brace of Martinis at
$1.60—or $2.00 in all for the two soused olives. Why didn't
Mr. Leiter add this to the indictment?

I'll tell you why: Because it wasn't the waiter's fault. And
so the waiter undoubtedly got his tip. Mr. Leiter knows you
can't blame the waiter for what's on his tray, if you ordered
it, any more than you can blame the newsboy for what's in the
paper. The moral is this: Raise Cain at the source. And if
you're going to stiff* one of the servitors, make sure it's the
one who gave you the trouble.

First, before we get into Who Gets Tipped How Much and
When, we'd better consider a few technical terms and some
generalities. These can best be handled, I think, by the Q. and
A. technique—a device which allows the writer to think up
questions no sensible person would really ask, so that the writer
can unload a lot of facts in his answers.

Q. *Must I tip even for slow, cross, sloppy service?*
A. No. Psychologists have a word for tipping under these
   circumstances. They call it "stupidity."
Q. *Why?*
A. Because it keeps the slow, cross, sloppy service going.

---

* STIFF: *transitive verb,* meaning not tipping someone who expects
you to; *noun,* any nontipper. STIFFERITIS: *noun,* meaning disease
characterized by stiffening of elbow and finger joints, making it
difficult if not impossible to reach into purse or pants pocket for
change.

Q. *What do I do when the hotel or the restaurant adds a 10% to 15% service charge to the bill, instead of a tip?*

A. You get yourself into a fine old sweat trying to decide what to do and end up tipping anyway, if you are like most people. You hate yourself for it, but you would feel worse if you didn't. That's why the system isn't working out, in Europe or anywhere else.

Q. *And when the fact of this 15% service charge is explicitly stated on menus and so forth, will the waiters and bellhops accept my tips anyway?*

A. Yes.* Next question.

Q. *In places where tipping is expected, and I don't tip, what will they do to me?*

A. They will call you names behind your back, but they're not allowed to hit you.

Q. *What kind of names?*

A. They'll probably call you a stiff. In some places they'll call you a fishball or a clutch or a snake or a lemon or a frog or a mossback.

Q. *What will they call me if I tip* BIG?

A. A mark. Or a live one.

Q. *Does that mean I'd get better service?*

A. Well, not necessarily. Some waiters and bellhops will knock themselves out trying to unstiff the stiffs.

Q. *Once I heard a bellboy call me a Sanitation Specialist. What did that mean?*

A. That meant you were hiding in the bathroom when he brought up your bags.

Q. *Oh.*

Now let's dispense with the gentleman in the back row and examine the basic coins of our currency and what they are good for.

THE NICKEL

Considered negotiable only by small children who run errands for you.

* But not if this is a private club, or a modest restaurant chain with blunt DO NOT TIP signs all over. These places do mean it.

THE DIME

For the shoeshine boy.

Also for the waitress—counter* or table—in a modest coffeehouse, tea shop, drugstore, or beanery, when the check totals less than 50¢.

A DIME AND A NICKEL

All right in those same places for a check between 50¢ and $1.

THE QUARTER

Now we're getting somewhere. You give a quarter to

Barbers, and *men's room attendants,* for handing you the towel that was right there, and *powder-room attendants,* for providing all those cosmetics you don't need. (If you do, give her 50¢. In any case, remember it's a miserable way to make a living.)

Hat-check girls. Some men weary of buying their hats back, though. I heard of a group of four who lined up, each saying to the man ahead, "I'll take care of it," and the last man left the quarter.

Redcaps, skycaps, 25¢ per bag (or more, depending on his grin and brand of service). By the way, it's wise to note his number. Then, if you've tipped him, say, $1 to put three bags on the train, and another redcap shows up with them at your seat, you may say, "I trust you're working in partnership with Number Seventeen, because he's the lad I just tipped for these."

Bellhops, in smaller cities, 25¢ per bag. In larger cities, 50¢, or three for $1. Same for any small service—fetching cigarettes, newspaper, et cetera, 25¢.

But you don't have to KEEP your hand in your change pocket. You can do this: When the bellhop takes up your bags, overtip him a dollar or two, saying, "I'll be around a few days and I'd like you to take care of me. What's your number, and when are you on duty?" Then ask for him whenever you call the desk, but don't tip him every time. The bellhop will hop, from a feeling of identity and personal responsibility, and a hunch that he'll be Taken Care Of when you check out. Which, of course, you'll see to. This doesn't save money, but it saves constant pungling and usually gets better service.

To continue, with who gets a quarter:

* Counter girls work just as hard, in narrower space, and they are usually responsible for more customers, and their feet get very sore.

Doorman, for getting a cab. But if he whistles you up a dozen a day, use the above bellhop system. Tip generously the first time, then skip it awhile.

Doorman, at a club restaurant, if he so much as opens the car door for you. If he so much as takes the car away and hides it somewhere and finds it again for you, it's 50¢ to $1, depending on the magnificence of the establishment and how many brandies you had.

Grocery delivery boy, unless there's a good thumping charge made for deliveries anyway. Or unless you give him a Christmas gift (page 60).

THE HALF DOLLAR

You give 50¢ to
Manicurists.

Hairdressers, for anything under a $4 check. Over that, figure 15%. If this is a salon instead of a shoppe, with pink silk smocks for the customers and free carrot juice, tip the shampoo girl 50¢, too, if she got you squeaky-clean. (If it is a more modest establishment with a separate shampoo girl, give her a quarter.)

Chambermaid, in a moderately priced hotel, 50¢ per night. Just leave it on the dresser in an envelope marked—logically enough—*chambermaid.* (In motels, you leave nothing for the chambermaid.)

THE ONE-DOLLAR BILL

Pullman porter, a dollar per night.

Chambermaid in luxury hotels, ditto.

Golf caddy, a dollar for 18 holes, where there is an additional caddy-service charge anyway, or 50¢ for nine. (Where there isn't a caddy-service charge, figure $4 for 18 holes, $2 for nine.)

Furniture mover. Give him two.

Then there are boats.

The simplest way is to figure 10% of your one-way boat fare. If your fare was $600, you have a $60. Tip Fund to divide among the dining-room steward, cabin steward, and deck steward. Just what you give whom depends on how much solicitude you've received from each. In the nature of things, the cabin steward is on more constant call than the others and therefore often gets a somewhat larger proportion of the Fund. (On the other hand, you may get a perfect gem of a deck steward, who does all sorts of nice things for you. So play it by ear.)

Whatever you decide, put the money in marked envelopes and hand it out the day before you dock. (Some people like to give half when they board the boat and the remainder on the last day. This, too, is your business.)

As for the bar steward, give him 15% of your bar bill—either each time you're presented with one or—if you charge it—all at once, at the end of the voyage.

Now, this 15% is, of course, the figure to remember whenever there's a tab involved.

Fifteen per cent of the meter is what you tip the cabbie, unless he has taken you from West 55th Street to West 56th Street via Newark, in which case you give your wandering boy no *Trinkgeld* whatsoever. If he is a cross cabdriver who sours the moment by not saying "Thank you" after you've tipped him, you can relieve your feelings by leaving the cab door ajar when you get out.

In some middle-sized cities, cabdrivers own their own cabs, paying a fixed monthly sum to the company whose name and facilities they use. These drivers make money whether they are tipped or not. Many charge-account customers in these cities do NOT tip. This is a comforting thing for parents to know who occasionally have little children transported by taxi—children too small to be trusted with change for tipping.

Fifteen per cent is what you tip anybody when you're in doubt.

Fifteen per cent is also the figure to cleave to—in spite of the gently swelling pressure on all fronts to up it to 20% (as it has already been upped in some places; see a little later on).

Fifteen per cent, moreover, brings us right back to the Bar and Grill. Let's take it from the top, in an average-to-good restaurant.

Bartender. Fifteen per cent—though in practice it's often more. For an 80¢ drink, you customarily leave the change from a $1 bill. (Clearly, it is expensive to fly on one wing; if you'd had two, totaling $1.60, you could properly leave a quarter, which is proportionately much less.) Also, if this is a good bar you consistently patronize through the year, the bartender will consider $5 a cheery Yuletide greeting.

NOTE: Women are expected to tip at bars, too—that is, in the states where women may legally sit at them. I thought of finding out just what states these are, but this was a lot of trouble. Anyway, in a different state, where you don't know the law, it's easy to ask the bartender or the waitress.

Actually, whether or not a woman should sit at a bar depends on the cut of her jib. If it is a wide one, it won't look so good on a bar stool, and she'd better take a table.

Bar girl or cocktail girl. In some restaurants, a cocktail girl —instead of the food waiter—brings you your drinks. She expects 15% and would prefer 20%, because those long black net stockings are expensive.

Waiter (or waitress). Fifteen per cent of the dinner or lunch check, always assuming the service has been good. If it has not, you leave nothing. By the way, there seems to be no satisfactory technique for getting good service from a bad waiter, though people have tried. A European millionaire named Nubar Gulbenkian tears a banknote in half, giving one part to his waiter and promising the other half if the service is good. A woman I know stacks quarters by her water glass the minute she's seated, then removes them one by one if things slow down. But, after all, these are bribes, and rather demeaning all around. Better just find another place to eat.

Now, that 15% should be upped, of course, if you hold down the table for hours. It must be remembered that the waiter's lot is not always a happy one. Indeed, he has several things to contend with.

THE WAITER'S DELIGHT

Technical term for the Wednesday Club that meets on Friday, makes no reservation, and shows up with six to 20 women who all order different lunches on one check, then conscientiously divide the total.

Most waiters, incidentally, regard women as terrible tippers. —Not stiffs, precisely, for a woman usually tries to cleave to the letter of the law. But she'll often shade it a bit. Like this:

The lunch check is $1.50. Well, 15% of that is . . . let's see . . . After arduous figuring, she comes up with 22½¢—a silly sum to tip anybody, not to mention impossible. And what's

2½¢? So she'll often leave 20¢, where a man will more often up it to 25¢, 35¢, or even 50¢, depending on where he is and whom he's impressing and the waitress's legs.

But as a philosophical waiter once explained it to me—and most good waiters are philosophers—women must nevertheless be warmly welcomed. It's so often the woman who decides on the restaurant when she goes out to dinner with a man.

And so to the expensive restaurant, the de luxe bistro, in the larger cities. This is a different situation. Here you can forget the 15% and think big. From 20% to 30%. Or, as ex-President Harry Truman once remarked, "If you can't stand the heat, stay out of the kitchen."

THE MAITRE D'HOTEL

*"You won't insult a maître d' by offering him money."**
—RAUL, of The Algonquin

Now, this is the man who can make you look good, with the perfect little dinner he helped you plan over the telephone, the cordial greeting, the choice table, and the commanding snap of the fingers that makes the henchmen jump.

But he expects to be paid for it.

In smaller cities he will make you look good for $2 or $3, which you give him, preferably, as you leave. (It is then a thank-you instead of a bribe. And I should think, although I have never been a maître d', that this would be the better psychology. He should be in a perfect lather throughout the time you're there, wondering what he's going to get.)

In the larger cities, it costs more to look good. For a party of six people, in a de luxe night club or an expensive restaurant, you would give him $5 to $10 at the door—always assuming, of course, that he made you happy.

Then there are the *waiter captain,* the *sommelier,* and the *bus boy.* But don't worry about the bus boy. The waiter pays him, 10% to 15% of his own tip.

In fact, don't worry about the other two, either. There are two things you can properly do:

* folding

1. You can specify who gets how much, if you care, by writing it on the check: $2 to the captain, $1 to the sommelier, et cetera. In this way you can reward the people who served you best.

2. Or you can do as most people do—just leave your rousing 20% to 30% tip with the waiter and specify nothing at all, hoping that it will all sort itself out, as it undoubtedly will.

Item: Twenty out of 100 people tip a maître d' who has done them no special service. Five out of 25 people tip the sommelier; 20 out of 100 people tip the headwaiter.

And now, having looked at the Tip Proper, let's take a brief look at the Tip Improper, or Tribute, or whatever you call the Christmas handout.

In a more innocent age, you could give people like the mailman or the apartment manager a nice box of homemade cookies for Christmas. Often you still can, if you live in Spongecake Falls. But in bigger cities, a certain steely-eyed commercialism has crept in. Apartment dwellers in a metropolis are often handed a list of names, complete with suggested amounts. And the Apartment Supe seldom reacts to your $10 bill with pretty cries of "Oh, but you *shouldn't* have!"

It goes like this:

Mailman, especially in New York City, $5 to $10, depending on the amount of mail. (But in many communities you give him nothing.)

Janitor or garbage collector, especially in New York City, $5. In other communities it's up to you, depending on the amount of your garbage and where you hide your cans.

Grocery delivery boy, $5, unless you tip him (see page 56).

Apartment-house superintendent, $5 to $20, depending on the city, the address, and the amount of service you expect. When you move in, ask the lady across the hall. Better still, ask her husband, who probably pays it.

Doorman. When your apartment house has a doorman all its own, he'll expect $10 to $15.

So, finally, to a few odd facts, some of them cheering.

There are some people you don't tip at all. *Airlines personnel,* except for skycaps. *Proprietors* of any shop or store. *Anyone you see socially* (for instance, your barber, if you go fishing with him). *Immigration officials,* for this would look like a bribe.

You are expected to tip more, incidentally, if you are wearing vicuña, chinchilla, or good mink—a fact that is cheering or not, depending on what's in your coat closet. This is the case unless your servitors know that you belong to the stingy aristocratic rich, who customarily tip the least. But if you do, you're probably wearing ratty old tweeds anyway (see Rich People, page 147).

New York and California are the top tipping places. It goes down a bit in the Midwest, and down a little bit more in New England and the deep South.

It is a good idea, by the way, to learn the economic facts of life in your own community, where tipping is concerned. In a highly unionized town, most waiters and waitresses expect and often get lower tips, because their salaries are fairly adequate.

Then, keep this in mind: At a hotel or resort, should you feel yourself getting dangerously twitchy from tipping so often, you can just take a deep breath and *stop*.

Tell the people, if you like, that you prefer to take care of these things when you leave. They may prefer it, too. If they are bright people, they will realize that constant tipping becomes hard on the disposition, and that by waiting they will probably do better in the long run.

You must remember, too, that some people still take a personal pride in giving good service, despite all the cynical things you hear. Some people don't *expect* to be tipped every time they open a door. (Don't let this concept run away with you, just keep it in mind.)

At any rate, you can take a certain philosophic comfort from the fact that if tipping stopped, wages would go up, and so would the price of everything. You know how it is. Lose it on the apples, make it up on the bananas, and that's the way the world goes.

> *"So thank your stars that matters are no worse,*
> *And read your Bible, Sir, and mind your purse."*
> —LORD BYRON

II

❋

THE WORD

"Zounds! I was never so bethump'd with words. . . ."
—SHAKESPEARE

CHAPTER FIVE

Excuse Me,
You're Standing on My
Status Symbol

*"I think quickly enough but I get behindhand
With what I ought to be saying. It's a kind of stammer
In my way of life, madam."*

—CHRISTOPHER FRY

In this chapter, if all goes well, we should come to grips with several problems pertaining mainly to conversation. We'll consider the matter of bores, and how to be reasonably courteous while comfortable. We'll touch on some perilous topics, some good words and some bad words, and some ways to pitch and field the compliment. Then, too, there'll be intermittent though respectful attention paid to the Social Lie; for Social Lies, now I think about it, seem to dart like minnows throughout this book. That is because they are important. Without the Social Lie, society pages would make livelier reading than they do, but life would be harder, and it is hard enough already. It is therefore important to be able to tell a Social Lie easily and well.

The subject of bores is one to be approached with diffidence and hedging, for, of course, it is true that nearly everyone occasionally bores someone else. It is only that some people are quicker than others to detect the glazed look in the eye of the listener.

You certainly can't say what subjects are dullest. Everyone has his own private list. Art, Annapolis, Antibes, Agee, Adolescence—you can name several for every letter in the alphabet, probably, depending on who you are, who's talking, and the mood you're in. And in some moods, anything will bore you.

Well, nobody ever said life was a six-ring circus with you clapping all the time. So, where good manners are concerned, the main thing is to perfect some techniques of getting away from bores, when this is at all possible (and to try to remember to intersperse one's own monologues with a few delightful flashes of silence, and hope for the best).

Let us consider the Homesteaders, who set up housekeeping beside you on the sofa, at a social gathering. You can see yourself growing old with the Homesteaders, going hand in hand into the sunset years with the Homesteaders. Yet you wouldn't hurt their feelings for the world.

This should be a lesson to you. Next time, *don't sit down on that sofa*. Or anywhere else, if you can avoid it. Be late to these things, for it's the early birds who get shoved into the nests; latecomers can stay on their feet.

If you do arrive early, perch with noticeable discomfort on a chair arm. This, admittedly, is a better move for a man than a woman. A kindly providence has provided that women look best from above. But in any encounter with the Homesteaders, mobility comes first.

In this situation, a woman can do this: She can look stricken, clutch hopelessly at a shoulder strap, and murmur, "I'm so sorry—*would* you excuse me?" Now she must head for the bathroom or the bedroom, but at any rate she has lifted anchor.

A man, too, can use the exclamation-and-mutter—possibly something about car lights or car keys. He must step outside then, but fresh air will taste good, and he can get lost coming back.

Either sex, of course, can remember the imperative phone call, or hunt for a nonexistent place to set a glass down, or for cigarettes, or for a book in the bookcase in the next room, exactly the Homesteaders' type. Or keep a sharp eye out for a replacement, and hail him cordially. If it is Charlie Snootful, already snockered, so much the better, for he won't see what's about to happen to him. Then all that is needed is a "Listen to this, Charlie—Homesteader, tell Charlie what you were just telling me. . . ."

Finally, there is a good maneuver which demands no props, only practice. It involves edging away on a rising burst of words which should sound like the start of a story but are actually an exit line. Talking with enthusiasm, often over one's shoulder, one moves purposefully away.

But sometimes you are faced with a bore at home: a television set, or a talkative in-law, or your friendly insurance man. These are stickier. Perhaps—for purposes of family unity —you feel it necessary to give eye service to a particular program. And you don't want to be rude to your guests.

The answer is *pickup work*, which has a long and honorable history. Many a Victorian lady staved off the whips and jingles in just this way. When the children had the pox, and the master of the house was being his lordly unlovable self, and her built-in mother-in-law never stopped talking, she didn't just sit around playing with her mental blocks. It was back to the old crewelwork (which, by the way, is having a nice revival).

And there are several things besides crewelwork a woman can do to keep her hands busy and her expression tranquil while her mind roams to far and greener meadows. She can make crazy-quilt cushion covers from her husband's old silk neckties. She can, of course, knit. She can crochet. She can even tat. And she can do petit point, which needn't end up on chair seats. She can make an evening purse or a spectacle case or a handsome huge carryall handbag, to be attached later to a tortoise-shell frame. (Most fair-sized department stores pay talented ladies to teach you how to do these things if you don't already know.)

Or, if all these seem pretty terrible, a woman can cover the lurid bindings of her good paperback books with self-sticking paper. Or keep a box of paper busywork handy—snapshots to be arranged in the family album, or clipped-out recipes to paste or file. And if all else fails, she can weave pot holders or place mats with the nylon loops and tiny looms—available at most variety stores—that are used for therapy in many mental hospitals.

Remember, it is better to have an hour of boredom and a couple of new pot holders than just an hour of boredom. And the sweeter you can keep your disposition, the better your manners are apt to be.

It is hard to think of pickup work for men, except for whittling, fly-tying, and building ships in bottles. But men don't seem to need it so much, for they are usually cavalier about leaving a room whenever the going gets thick.

As we noted earlier, it's hard to make any sensible flat-footed statements about what subjects are dull. More rewarding is a brisk look at some that are best avoided for other reasons. —Not because they are controversial (for, of course, people who go around avoiding controversial topics might as well get back into their playpens), but because they might hurt someone's feelings, which is nearly always bad manners, or make one look foolish.

For instance, *Age*.

Age is a truly perilous topic with both men and women alike. Some people count each birthday pridefully, like another Purple Heart, but some—on the other hand—don't. Therefore, it is unwise to say "people our age" unless you're certain your new acquaintance graduated with you, or unless you're sure he is vastly older than you are. "Middle-aged" is also a dangerous word, being wide open to personal interpretation. Some people wait longer than others to strike their colors.

Because of this, a woman should be careful about giving up her seat in a public conveyance to a woman she considers older. Maybe the other woman doesn't regard herself that way, and this could spoil her week. Shoes are a good clue. If she is wearing reasonably high, slender heels, let her stand. If she has settled now for honest arch supports, give her your seat.

Bodily Ailments These are bad conversational fodder, for

two reasons. Here, indeed, dullness often enters. It is truly breathtaking how many people don't want to get acquainted with your gall bladder.* (Of course, you can tell intimate friends about it, with color slides if you like, but it isn't advisable in general company.) More important, when a new acquaintance discusses these intimate matters that acquaintance is marked forever after in your mind as "the man with the bile duct" or "the lady with the feet."† I know an attorney whom I can never see without thinking of his kidneys. This is because of an evening when, as his dinner partner, I was treated to an unforgettable tour of his urinary tract. Had he thought about it, I'm sure he wouldn't have wanted to live in my mind in quite this way.

A good name for what is the matter with you—when something obviously is but you don't care to say what—is a term often used in religious communities: *"petites misères."* This covers any of those small, slightly revolting bodily infirmities which you'd generally prefer to leave unspecified.

(Similarly, you needn't be truthful when someone asks how you got the lump on your head. You may quite properly say you were wounded at karate practice, which has more dignity than bumping into the bathroom door.)

Children The situation here is this: Some people's children are outstanding, and some are what might be called instanding; that is, they stand in well with the family and the group but will probably set no worlds afire once they're turned loose.

It is bad manners to brag about an outstanding child to other mothers, who may not be blessed with one. Their feelings will be hurt—far more than if you'd bragged about your bank account, which could be laughed off as merely gauche. But maternal pride is understandable, which makes it all the harder

---

* Or your mental traumas, blocks, and psychoanalyst. A person's first analysis in depth is rather like a woman's first pregnancy. One tends to consider one's condition extraordinarily interesting, not quite realizing how many times it has happened before, to other people. A safe rule is that those pregnant should talk pregnancy only with others equally pregnant, and people undergoing deep therapy should stick to others similarly occupied.

† It is a curious thing, by the way, that the expression "my foot hurts" sounds ladylike, but "my feet hurt" doesn't.

to bear. Then, too, with the population exploding as it is, you may some day produce an instanding child yourself.*

Nor should a wife brag about her husband, even though she married a true pearl. This bores other wives and also has them suspecting that the lady doth protest too much.

Décor A good topic to stay away from, at least until you've seen each other's quarters. Your Upper Bohemian friend may be pained right down to the soles of his chukka boots by your Early Williamsburg living room, and you may think his African masks are early Halloween. But if neither of you has made any snide remarks beforehand, no harm has been done.

Many a budding friendship has been blighted by one blithe remark about "green-stamp modern" or "deviationist Eames" or "cozy-wozy Victorian" or "*you* know, *maple* people." This is too bad, for the followers of all these schools have their virtues. Many maple people know the outdoors, and Victorians often know books, and green-stamp people usually pay their bills, and the Eames group are often inventive cooks. These are all points to be considered.

Status Symbols Here, too, is an area paved with eggshells. One problem is that you are not always sure exactly what someone's status symbol is. The possibilities are many. It may be a game, like polo or no-limit stud poker. Or an attitude, like hating one's psychiatrist and loving one's pharmacist. Or an arduously acquired habit, like using only French walnut oil in the dressing for green salads. Or a possession, like a 1914 Stutz-Bearcat. Or a lack of a possession, like having no television set.

Any one of these can be redolent of status in one section of the country, and just plain redolent in another. It is hard to think of a status symbol—with the possible exception of getting a 21-gun salute every time you go somewhere—that can't be one-upped by someone else or outdated by tomorrow, or adopted by so many people that you must move on to another.

For this reason, incidentally, when adopting a status symbol,

---

* A wise young husband once dissuaded his wife from bringing the baby downstairs to show to a group from the office. "Don't show the baby off, honey," he said "Everyone here either has one or hasn't."

it is wise to choose one you really like, so that when its status value wears off, you still don't mind having it around (or not having it around, as in the case of the TV). This is especially true when it is an expensive possession. You can easily stop ordering that walnut oil from France, but it's not so simple to pretend that the Stutz-Bearcat never happened, or the polo team.

It is because of its evanescent nature that one must be respectful or, at the least, noncommittal about someone else's status symbol once one has discovered what it is.

"Where was there easier work, ever, than shutting the mouth?"
           —OVID

And now, before we proceed, a word about words. Much attention is being paid to them these days—to good words and bad words, U words and non-U words, highbrow, middlebrow, and superbottombrow words.

The rule for good words, of course, is to use the reasonably basic word, rather than the word that's prettied up. This rule, like most rules, must be tempered with sense. A friend of mine taught her small son the physiological names for simple bodily functions that don't deserve so many syllables, and the first time the little boy tried to explain his needs at the gas station, the attendant was drop-jawed.

However, in general, the rule applies.

Some of the words in the following list are open to argument. Locale, custom, moment, and tradition have something to do with these things (just as addressing a woman as "Ma'am" sounds servile in some situations but is correct in others). No list of this kind could possibly be complete, for the good words all stem from an at-home-in-the-world state of mind which accepts a fact as a fact. And there's many a fact in this world which can be either faced or glossed over.

POOR WORDS	GOOD WORDS
beauty shop, beautician	hairdresser
bosoms*	breasts

* Unless it is a sentence like "The women clasped them to their bosoms." Otherwise, one bosom usually equals two breasts.

POOR WORDS	GOOD WORDS
boudoir	bedroom (unless boudoir is literally meant)
Cad, Caddy*	car
davenport	sofa
den	workroom, office, study
dentures	false teeth
formal, formal gown	long dress, evening dress
foundation garment	corset, girdle
funeral director	undertaker
genteel, refined	well-bred
gone, we lost him, passed away	dead, he died
hose, hosiery	stockings
inebriated	drunk
in the family way	pregnant
lady dog, lady horse	bitch, mare
launder	wash
little girl's room, john, johnny	bathroom, toilet
maiden lady	unmarried woman, spinster
mortician	undertaker
panties	underpants
,pardon?	what? or what did you say?
perspire	sweat
position	job
rumpus room	play room
Senior Citizens, Golden Yearlings	old people, older people
shoot your cookies, etc.	vomit, throw up
tails	white tie
The Man Upstairs	God
tummy	stomach, belly
tuxedo	black tie
veranda	porch
wealthy	rich

* A woman once volunteered to pick up a friend in the Cad, but her friend said No, she'd take the Plym.

Next, to a few conversational niceties and small problems.

Conversational Crosscurrents. Often, in a group of four, A and B are discussing something interesting, but C—who is sitting beside you—will neither listen nor let you. Thus, there are two loud duets instead of a conversation. It is wholly permissible in this case to lean forward with rapt attention toward A and B, murmuring to C, "Excuse me, but I think we just missed something fascinating!" It doesn't always work, but it's worth a try.

The Impulsive Confider Sometimes an overburdened soul will confide, all unasked, that she weighs 142 pounds and has an uncle in jail for car-stealing (or other items equally personal). Proper etiquette does not oblige you to confide back. You are privileged to reply, simply, "Fancy that!"

Then, too, there is the family backbiter—usually a brand-new female acquaintance—who deposits in your lap a load of unpleasant tidbits about her husband and the rest of her family. The only workable response to this is "How interesting, but I don't believe a word of it!" (even though you do). This helps shorten the conversation, and it may keep her from hating herself in the morning.

The Fifty-Cent Word When someone mispronounces a word which you must use shortly thereafter, it's kinder to choose a synonym. But there are few synonyms for some words, like "Freud," and you needn't say "Frood" because someone else did. He will probably think the mispronunciation is yours, anyway.

The Cut Direct This is bad form, and—worse—it's bad tactics. It shows your adversary how much you're bleeding. Therefore, whether she stole your color scheme or your spouse, the way to greet her is with a shrewd mixture of barely concealed amusement and solicitude. She will then get the uneasy hunch that you know something *she* doesn't.

Which brings to mind those people who remark, "Now I'm a person who always says just what I think." But these people seldom think anything pleasant. They think, "That so-called best friend of yours is a trollop, let's face it," and then they say it.

You may respond, with gentle courtesy, "I know her far

better than you do, and I know you're mistaken." Or you may say, "Thank you for your interest—I know she will appreciate it." Or if you like more catsup on your conversation, you may say, "Well, it takes one to know one," and go on to other matters.

As we shall go, now, to the pleasanter pastures of The Compliment, which is a lovely thing. Yet, so often, it is better to give than to receive, unless the compliment-giver really knows what he is about. For one thing, he'll often go doggedly on, while the complimentee scuffs the toe of one shoe over the other, and scuffs, and scuffs.

A compliment should be brief, and should contain a conversational hook. Like, "What a good-looking suit! Did you find it in San Francisco?" (Personal compliments used to be Out, but now they are In, and a good thing, too. Since Adam and Eve, no one ever really objected to hearing he looked good when he did.) The complimentee can then say a simple "Thank you—yes, we had a fine trip there," which will take care of the situation nicely. (There's no need to complain about how the skirt fits, or the fact that you're not sure about the color.)

Now, the *delayed* compliment is good. It proves the thing really registered.

And the word "always" is good, for it makes a compliment go farther.

But the word "little"—except when it is applied to a woman's waistline—can be dangerous. *I love your little place, little car, the little book you wrote.* Maybe his 100 x100 lot looks big to him. Maybe he thinks he drives a *big* car, wrote a *big* book.

Then there is the compliment with fallout.

Like the eleven-year-old boy, forced to escort his twelve-year-old cousin to a dance. His parents insisted that he pay her a courtly compliment, too, and so he did his best. For a girl as overweight as she was, he told her, she sure didn't perspire very much.

And consider:

"Your hair is graying so becomingly!"

"That's a lovely Rousseau print of yours, and it's getting so popular now, too!"

"I love that dress on you—it's especially good for your type of figure."

"I'm glad you're having another baby—you're so *relaxed* with your children." (Big Fertility Symbol. Earth Mother.)

Or "You have a new hairdo. I like it *so* much better!"—which, of course, has her wondering how on earth she must have looked before. It's better to say, "You're looking even prettier than usual." That is, if you more or less mean it, which is important. For a compliment should assay at least 60% truth to 40% geniality or it is hardly worth giving.

Otherwise, it can cause you trouble, too. For instance, if you overpraise your hostess's French fried haggis ("absolutely the best in the world"), you may well hurt the feelings of a female guest who French fries a pretty mean haggis herself, which you may have eaten. And if you keep on stressing its excellence when you honestly don't like it, you'll probably be faced with it the next time you dine there, and the next time, and the next. The sins ye do by two and two, ye pay for, one by one.

And, of course, too many compliments are really worse than not enough. For no one believes the person who barges about complimenting everything in sight, and he's gone to all that trouble for nothing.

"Certainly moderate praise, used with opportunity and not vulgar, is that which doth the good."   —FRANCIS BACON

CHAPTER SIX

Let It Ring, Let It
Ring, Let It Ring

*"For the last five—no, ten—years he'd
been holding out his day like a live target
for anybody to shoot full of holes."*
—DAWN POWELL

Some etiquette books talk at length about telephone manners
without getting down to fundamentals, like the fact that it's unwise to press the telephone to your rib cage while making a
frank aside to someone in the room. Nearly always, this can
be heard at the other end of the line. It is even risky to cover

75

the receiver with your hand, although you might experiment. I believe it depends on how thick your hand is.

How telephone sounds carry is mysterious, anyway. For instance, if there's so much noise at your end of the line that you can't hear, cover the mouthpiece—not your unemployed ear—and you'll hear better. You'll hear better still if you'll get the children out of the room.

This brief chapter will include telephone etiquette points of this practical type, which haven't been mentioned or stressed enough elsewhere. Social Lies will reappear, for they are so often necessary over the telephone. And there will be, of course, a few simple basics for both the caller and the callee.

The Big Three for the telephone caller are
1. to give his name immediately (because most people have telephone guessing games), and
2. to ask immediately thereafter if this is a convenient time to talk, and
3. to come to the point.

Of these, Number 2 is most often overlooked, which is surprising when you think of the many rather uninterruptible things one does in the course of a day. And not asking disconcerts the polite telephonee, who—caught off guard—can't always think of a courteous way to break in and break off.

I know a polite woman who uses a minute-minder to good advantage, in this situation. She keeps it by the telephone. When the telephone rings, she immediately sets the minute-minder for three minutes. The caller can hear it when it rings, of course, and the woman says, "Heavens, I must pick up Edward!" (or phone the doctor, or feed the baby, or whatever logical-sounding Social Lie comes to mind).

Another ruse is to start panting, at the first ring of the telephone, and answer with a windy "I was just going out the door!"

Also, when a telephoner bursts in upon you, full flood, with a total-recall account of her day and the day before that, with never a by-your-leave, there is nothing at all the matter with a briskly courteous "I'm so sorry—I can't talk now. May I call you later, at a better time?"

As for Number 3 in our basic rules for telephoners, the caller must come to the business at hand promptly, so that the callee may don the proper hat with no fumbling. If your caller doesn't do this, the conversation limps along and you tend to limp along with it—after all, something pleasant, some exciting invitation, may be in the offing. And perhaps, with this unworthy thought in mind, you show more cordiality than you otherwise would. But then, when the boom is lowered, and you're invited to head the Clean-up Squad for the Rummage Sale, the notion is even more depressing than it would have seemed in the first place.

In this day of perfectly ghastly long seven-eight-and-nine-digit telephone numbers, the caller had better look up the number, no matter how well he thinks he knows it. My town's 375,000 people—and they're as bright as most people, too—manage to dial 70,000 wrong numbers every day. The frustration implicit here—multiplied by all the other towns across the country—is enough to start another Civil War, and if there's anything the country doesn't need right now, it's that.

Another thing: In this day of direct distance dialing, not looking up numbers can be expensive. If you misdial the area code number while aiming for Texas, you could land in New England, and end up paying for it, too. (Should this ever happen, dial your operator immediately and explain the situation. Otherwise, that unrewarding chat with some Brattleboro bartender may well show up on next month's bill.)

So, if you frequently make telephone calls away from the house or office, it's wise to sit down, some rainy day, and laboriously copy out all the most frequently called numbers in your telephone index, including long-distance ones. Then you carry the booklet in your pocket or purse.

Furthermore, the telephone caller must keep in mind the point of no return (or point after which you can't politely turn back). The point of no return, in making a telephone call, is the second ring of the phone. After that, the caller can't change his mind and decide not to call you after all. He must see this thing through to the bitter end. After all, he's already sprung you out of the bathtub, and if that phone stops ringing while you're in mid-flight, your blood pressure is going to rise. The fact that you'll never know who did this to you makes it even worse, and he'd just better not do it, or it will be another freckle on his soul, and who needs more? Indeed, proper etiquette says that he must let that telephone ring 12 times—which is one minute. This gives you time to dry your back and find your cigarettes.

Then one more thing: Coming in cold on your situation, as

does every telephoner, being a dropper-inner or butter-inner whenever he makes a phone call, he'd better not start the conversation right out with a merry ha-ha quip or a boolah-boolah. It's best to take the emotional temperature of the callee first. There could be grievous trouble at the other end of the line, and the caller could feel silly.

Next, about the telephone answerer:

A big thing for him to remember is that he doesn't *have* to answer. This is stressed, because people tend to forget it. They take expensive trips to get away from the telephone, and they exhaust themselves searching for their own personal Walden Ponds, when they could have a pool of quiet at home through the simple expedient of not answering.

Remember, now: It is perfectly good manners not to, even though it's the lady across the street who is calling you and she *knows* you're home because she can *see* you, through her big fat picture window. In Grandmother's day, a maid or a hired girl sent away unwelcome visitors with a "Madam is not at home" or "The Missus ain't here," as the case might have been. But since the invention of the telephone and the disappearance—for most of us—of the dragon at the door, the simplest way of guarding one's privacy is through not answering the telephone.

If it is important, the caller will try again. Even if it isn't he will, and you'll still have a chance to win that free dancing lesson by naming the first President of the United States.

Another thing: It's often better not to answer on those days when the telephone has been a shrilling banshee and you are, as a result, on edge, for you might forget your manners. And it's important to be kind to the little voices selling hospital insurance and coupon books; maybe the dreary work is the only kind they can do, or do at home.

One time you should answer, though, is this: Say your telephone rings and rings at 3:00 A.M., and you've neither friend nor enemy who's apt to call you at this unlikely time. Let it wear itself out, the first time, for it's probably somebody wanting Eddie's Steak House. But if it starts again, after a short pause, it could be long-distance, or otherwise urgent.

How to Make the Telephone Less Irritating   Phone jacks are helpful, because you can simply unplug them. There'll be a ring in the basement or somewhere, because the telephone company's rule says there has to be, but it will be only a far-away buzz. Also, most modern telephones can be dialed to LOW. You can do this and then put a pillow over it. Or, if your telephone has an ill-natured ring, you can have a bell chime installed (for an installation fee of about $5, plus 65¢ a month in addition to your standard charge).

If you hate being lashed to the mast as you talk, you can get a shoulder rest and a 25-foot cord and roam to the end of your tether. (I understand that the telephone company now discourages the use of long cords because people can trip over them. But you can trip over rugs and everything else, too, for heaven's sake. I've had a long cord for ten years and haven't tripped yet.) Or you can get a speaker phone, which you can talk into from any point in the room, for $13 for installation, plus $7.50 per month in addition to your regular charge. But if you have hordes of committee meetings at your house, or if your whole family likes to talk all at once to Grandma, it might be worth it, though hard on Grandma.

Then there's the matter of ruining your manicure while dialing. Fancy little dialers, from any gift shop, will solve this, and so will a five-cent pencil. So will the new card-index phone into which you tuck prepunched cards, and you never have to dial again; $3.50 extra per month, plus $15 to install.

All these things, or any one of them, can help keep you better-tempered, you see, which will automatically improve your etiquette.

About Answering   In answering a business telephone, it's best to skip the cheery "Good morning" that's often tacked to the end of the firm name. This can throw the caller off his pace. He was all set for a businesslike "Mr. Mel McLemore, Sales Promotion, please," but now he must switch hats and say "Good morning" right back, or feel churlish. (A friend of mine had an upsetting experience in Ireland. Calling Rooney & Muldoon Car Rental Service, he was greeted with "Rooney and Muldoon Car Rental Service, sure and it's a grand immortal day!" which was such a grand immortal thought that my friend couldn't remember what he was calling about.)

The business telephone answerer must be particularly careful about his tactics in answering the phone for someone else. When you call Mr. McLemore's office and ask his secretary for Mr. McLemore, she mustn't ask, "Who's calling, please?"

and when, when you say *you* are, tell you that he isn't in. It sounds like a lie, whether it is or not, and makes you feel small and unloved. Instead, she must say, "I'm sorry, he isn't in now. May I have your name so he can call you?" Or, if McLemore is a very busy man who doesn't take just any old phone call, she can lie politely with an "I'll see if he's back yet—may I have your name, please?" Then she can protect his privacy and your feelings all at once. (Admittedly, you got off on the wrong foot in the first place. Had you said, "This is Tish Kabibble, may I speak to Mr. McLemore?" you would have avoided the whole problem.)

"Hello" is the correct way to answer the telephone at home, although a simple "Yes?" will do, if you can give it the properly cordial, rising note. Alexander Graham Bell recommended "Ahoy" or "Hoy hoy," which has rather a bracing effect, but it tends to confuse people. *And if your caller should riposte with "Who's this?" you are privileged to replace the receiver gently upon its cradle.*

If, in answering, you want to hurry things along, or if you happen to answer the telephone in someone else's house, you may properly say "Drydens' house." —*Not* "Drydens' residence." This, by the way, is a good thing to teach children. A wee piping voice is better than nothing, if it isn't talking about teddy bears, and even a very small child can learn to answer the telephone in this fashion.

On Identifying Yourself   A man, identifying himself, simply says, "John Dryden." An unmarried girl or woman does likewise: "Johanna Dryden." And so does a married woman, when she is making a social call or receiving one. "This is Johanna Dryden," she says, not "Mrs. John Dryden." However, her saying this is not, of course, an invitation to first-name her; it's just her social identification. To the plumber or the grocer she'd say, "Mrs. John Dryden," because her married name is more impersonal and probably better known to the plumber and to the store.

One other point here: A woman's age used to affect the way she gave her name on the telephone. For reasons of dignity, Mrs. Pushing Seventy would call herself just that, when she gave her name to younger friends and acquaintances. But she doesn't do it so much any more, and certainly needn't, unless she wants to. After all, a woman's first name is her first name, whether she's 19 or 97, and she can use it on the telephone all her life, if she likes, as she does in her letters.

Teen-agers and Telephones One partial tranquilizer for this situation is a separate telephone for them. I know some parents who paid the initial installation charge, then let the teen-agers baby-sit the monthly payments. They found that other teen-agers kept calling them, on the parental phone, to ask them to tell the teen-agers to get off theirs so they could call them, if you follow this. But on the whole, they say, it helps.

Now just a few miscellaneous points of telephone etiquette.

When you visit friends in another city and make a few calls on the assumption that they're local, or free, it's good manners to make sure. City and suburban arrangements differ. Also, your host may have a limited-service setup, which charges for local calls over a specific number. Leaving him with all those fifteen centses to pay is a small chisel that one probably wouldn't want to perpetrate. Now, it's true that most people feel awkward about accepting a piddling 15¢ (although a walloping $12 long-distance call is something else again). So the best solution is to get yourself a telephone-company credit card. Then the call is automatically charged to you, no matter whose telephone you used.

Party lines are something to avoid if you can possibly make another arrangement. The only person who benefits from them is the marathon talker, who doesn't want to admit she is. She can blame that perpetual busy signal, so annoying to her friends and her husband, on the other party. However, if you do tangle with a party line, it's good to remember not to dial first without listening; not to make ten calls in a row, but to wait five minutes after each; and always to relinquish the line if someone needs it for an emergency call. For one thing, it's only decent, and for another, you may find yourself in court with a weak case. In many states, not giving up the line under these circumstances is a misdemeanor.

A marvelous device, by the way, for saving time while keeping posted on your friends is the prearranged lunch-time phone call, if you're both on one-party lines. Instead of meeting for lunch, which takes time, bother, and money, you can lunch separately at home, with the wire hot between you, and cover fully as much ground.

Another good thing to know is the Magic Number. This is

the number you can dial which makes your own telephone ring. Perhaps your telephone company will give it to you. Or maybe the telephone repairman will. And many teen-agers know it, for they absorb this sort of information through the pores.

At any rate, it is convenient to know. It makes magic for little children, for it enables you to give more verisimilitude to your conversations with Santa Claus and the Tooth Fairy. A teen-age girl finds it helpful, too, in making herself look sought after when she has guests. (She stops en route to the kitchen, rings the telephone, then giggles she's sorry, Friday night's taken, Saturday's gone . . . isn't it Grimsville!) And grown-ups can use it handily, to escape from sticky situations. Should a drop-in guest stay too long (or an invited one, for that matter), any loyal spouse can and will disappear for a moment, ring the phone, and reappear with dire reports of drop-in relatives waiting at the airport, or whatever bit of invention comes to mind. This is very practical etiquette, for it solves a problem but hurts no feelings.

And so to the *Social Lie*. Here, as in so many areas, I can fairly lay claim to as much ineptness as the next person. Yet hindsight is a great teacher. I have seen clearly, so many times, what I should have done. Additionally, it has been my privilege, on occasion, to watch good social liars at work over the phone.

For instance, take the proper telephone handling of the Vague Invitation.

Mrs. Meanswell telephones you with a cordial, nearly breathless "Are you busy Friday night?"—a question no one should ask, yet people do. Obviously, you can't say you're not. Her next line might be, "Then *do* come to our little girl's piano recital—she's playing 'Amaryllis!' " On the other hand, the Meanswells—as you happen to know—occasionally give good theater parties, with champagne after the show and all sorts of jazzy goings on. So you can't say you ARE busy.

What you say, with a harried note, is this: "Really, I wish I knew! We've an awful duty thing hanging over us that I'm expecting a call about, any minute." This is known as Hand-forcing. Unless she is totally obtuse, Meanswell will have to show her cards. If it's a Royal Flush, you can call her back in half an hour with the glad news that you've squiggled out of your obligation. If it turns out to be "Amaryllis" after all, you've still a way out.

The second technique, equally helpful, is the big No, buttressed by the fuzzy lie and the fast elision—of great value in getting out of jobs you don't want to do.

Often, in this world, the spirit is willing but the flesh can't stand any more. Busier than six people anyway, you are wondering if there'll ever be time to improve your forehand, or get acquainted with the kids or your immortal soul, or do some of the things that are sinful or slothful or fattening or all three, but that at any rate must be done occasionally for any sort of well-balanced regime. And here comes another job, usually over the phone because the caller is ashamed to look you in the eye.

You mustn't do it, that's all. Instead, you do this:

1. You say a positive NO, spiked with amazement—a note of "you can't mean this seriously!"

2. You follow it swiftly with a fuzzy reason why. Housefuls of guests or a doubled office load are all right, though not as foolproof as a good physical ailment. In this situation you can forget the *petites misères* on page 68. It's secondary that you're pegged as the one with the liver, just so you're pegged as the one to leave alone. So it's good to have an ailment handy, even though you must invent one. And, by the way, backs are in now. You can mention "that trick back of mine" or your old back trouble, even though the only trouble it ever caused you was affording clothes to put on it. No matter. Just don't be too specific.

3. Then, lightning swift with never a comma, you move the subject away from yourself: ". . . this miserable back of mine and I know you can find someone *dependable* to sort the underwear for the bazaar and isn't it great the enthusiasm everyone's showing about the new gym?" Just keep moving and stay out of the clinches.

This, then, is the technique. Of course, it takes practice. But is there anything truly worth-while that doesn't?

". . . I fought a war with conscience; and I won it. I always win."   —MORRIS BISHOP

CHAPTER SEVEN

Dear Sir, or Madam, as the Case May Be

". . . Never sprinkle French, Italian, or any other foreign words through a letter written in English unless the foreign word has no English equivalent, or has become anglicized. . . ."
—The New Emily Post's Etiquette

". . . In fact, if you want, you can interject almost anything in a foreign tongue . . . and what in English might be considered crude becomes in another language at least bearable."
—Amy Vanderbilt's New Complete Book of Etiquette

". . . Business letters usually end up with 'Very truly', 'Yours very truly', or 'Very truly yours', but not 'Yours truly.' . . ."
                                    —EMMA AUBERT COLE, The Modern Bride Book
                                           of Etiquette and Entertaining

"The close of a business letter should be 'Yours truly.' . . ."
                                    —The New Emily Post's Etiquette

Listen to the sounds of battle! Hear the clash of tiny swords! You have a choice, you see, depending on your allegiance. You can spike your letter or not with foreign words, and you can close it with any number of dull ones.

Also—a fact the experts don't mention—you can more or less do as you like. *Merde alors!* It's your letter!

Then there are some other facts they leave alone.

Personal Letters   The big thing about the personal letter is not to answer it too soon. When you do, you're only keeping a clear conscience at the expense of somebody else's, as someone has said—probably Thoreau, who seems to have said most of the best things.

There are two kinds of people: *lettrophiles,* who adore writing letters and receiving them, and *lettrophobes,* who hate to write letters and don't much care if they get any or not, except for love letters and letters with checks enclosed. For some reason, lettrophiles usually pick on lettrophobes, which eventually proves disconcerting to them both.

When you hate to write letters, it is important never to promise to, unless you and your friend share a big, all-absorbing mutual interest. The last thing you want to do is write chatty letters about your daily round, and the second-to-last thing you want to do is hear about hers.

The moment of truth is the moment a letter-lover moves away, saying, "I'll write and *you answer me.*" "I can't guarantee a thing," you must mumble, shamefacedly but loudly enough to be heard. This is difficult, but necessary. Otherwise, you're letting yourself in for the misery of writing letters, or the equal misery of not writing them and feeling bad about it. For good manners rightly insist that one answer one's mail.

You should own more post cards than writing paper. You can have your monogram die stamped on good-looking thick white cards—the larger the monogram the better, for it will leave less room to write on. (Small fold-over informals share this virtue, to a point, but they still have more writing surface.) You can use these post cards for invitations, too, as well as general correspondence.

Another thing: Letter-haters should consider the advantages of the tape recorder. Should your parents, for instance, live in a distant city and want you to write to them occasionally, as many parents seem to do, you might invest in two tape-recorder setups—one for you and one for them—at about $75 apiece. The whole family can help fill up the tape, before you mail it, to be played at the other end. (This has special advantages for fond grandparents, who'd like to *hear* the baby learning to talk.)

Now, if you like to write letters, it is dubious manners to write very often to people who don't. When you feel a nearly irresistible urge to write, lie down a few minutes until it passes away, or take a short walk.

Also, at the end of most notes, put the initials N.R.S.V.P., which mean, of course, *"Ne répondez, s'il vous plaît,"* or "Don't answer, please." This is an extremely thoughtful thing to do, for, without being rude, it takes the recipient off the hook. Its full translation is, "Don't answer, please (unless of course you feel like it), for I know how busy you are and how much you hate to write letters. —I just thought this little item might amuse you." All this, mind you, is implicit in those five initials. I know a well-bred woman who does this often. She likes to send thoughtful notes and clippings to her friends, but she doesn't want them to feel obliged to answer.

Letter-haters should use N.R.S.V.P., too, on the rare occasions when they do write. These people are often more thoughtful than you'd think, and they would write thoughtful notes more often if they weren't afraid of starting something.

A frequent problem with constant letter-writers is that when they run out of friends to write to, they find themselves writing Letters to the Editor. Presently they find themselves getting more mail than even *they* want to answer (because people are violently in favor of or opposed to their ideas on the new viaduct or whatever).

The solution to this, or to any situation in which you're getting too much mail, some of it angry, is *printed post cards*.

You have a gross printed as follows:

> Dear Sir or Madam,
> > You may be right at that.
> > > Sincerely,
> > > (Whatever your name is)*

Now a word about personal letters in general. There are four things to beware of:

1. Never send a letter in an envelope marked *Personal* to someone's house, for it implies that he has a snoopy family. (If you think he does, send the letter to his office.)

2. Never send carbon copies of a personal letter to anyone but family—unless you're on a big exciting trip and someone has *asked* you to. Some people do this to friends, especially at Christmas, but with the first carbon it ceases to be a personal letter and becomes a bore.

3. Never omit your address from the writing paper itself, even though the return address is on the envelope. Many people toss envelopes away automatically, and they may have no way of finding you again. (If the lady who sent me the handsome pink-painted whisky bottle should read these lines, this is the reason you never heard from me. Your address should have been on the whisky bottle or the note which accompanied it. It is a lovely whisky bottle, though, and thank you.)

4. If your old buddy lives in Chicago and your new buddy is going there, and you are flooded by that spirit of bonhomie which occasionally overcomes us all, write to your old buddy and tell him your new one will be in town, and when, and that he'll be staying at the Festered Arms. *But don't tell your new buddy you wrote.* Should his phone ring, it will come as a delightful surprise, but you will not have put your old buddy on the spot—a wicked thing to do to any old buddy.

Now. What to write personal letters *on.*

---

* Stewart Holbrook, the well-known historian, uses these cards and told me their origin. In the early 1930's, when H. L. Mencken was editing *The American Mercury,* Mr. Holbrook was in Mencken's office, telling him and George Jean Nathan about some of the insulting mail he'd been getting, and that it bothered him. Mencken frowned and said, "Got a pencil? Now take this down. Be sure you get it right or don't use it at all." Stewart Holbrook got it right and has used it ever since.

The simplest thing to do—and no etiquette expert can fault you for it—is to buy a big batch of good-quality writing paper —white, cream, or pale gray, airmail weight or standard, seven inches by nine inches, which is a good ambisextrous size— with matching envelopes.

(This is assuming you want to be charming or impress somebody. Actually, though, the best letters I've ever received were written by people who were more interested in what they were writing than what they were writing *on,* and usually they were typed on newsprint or on plain white second sheets that cost $1.50 a ream. Then they were folded twice and stuck into long airmail envelopes—the kind you buy prestamped at the post office. These were as pedigreed people as you'd ever care to meet, too, some of them with degrees out to *here.* So it goes to show that the etiquette people should get their noses out of the clouds, once in a while, and look around, and see what's going on.)

But back to being charming: You have these seven- by nine-inch sheets now, so leave some of it blank* for second pages, then have the rest engraved or printed with your address *only,* so the whole family can use it. Whether it is engraved or printed depends on your finances, the formality of your general correspondence, and whether or not your friends run their thumbs over the letterheads. Spell out everything there's room for. In the etiquette books' examples, there's always room for the whole thing:

Burnished Oaks . . . . Dark Island . . . . Mystic, Connecticut

But many addresses read more like

2418 Skinker Boulevard, Apt. #18
St. Louis 32, Missouri

In these cases you must use your own judgment.

Also, unless your correspondence is more formal than most people's, it's convenient to have your telephone number included on your personal letterhead. You find it there more and more often, in this day of direct distance dialing.

If your return address is printed on the envelopes, the Post

---

* Or all of it, if you want to. The most formal paper needn't have a word on it.

Office wants it done on the face, in the left-hand corner. Etiquette purists prefer it on the back flap. You must decide where your loyalties lie.

Anything except an answer to a third-person invitation (see page 155) can be properly written on a typewriter today, if you type better than you write. This is true even of letters of condolence. It would be poor manners indeed to send an indecipherable note to someone in time of grief.

Many people make their M's, N's, I's, R's, and E's all alike, which is smart-looking but illegible. If you write like this,

no one but you will ever know that Mimi needs a minimum muumuu, and you'd have done far better to type it.

Also, many people today have been trained early to the typewriter, and *think* better on the typewriter, which makes for a better letter.

It is a nice affectation, however, to write the salutation by hand—the "Dear Jane"—before typing the rest.

It is kinder to your correspondent to forget the old nonsense about numbering your pages 1, 3, 2, 4, if your paper is the folded sort with four sides. Some wild-eyed old lady in the Social Register got fouled up one day and did this, I believe, and somebody rationalized a reason for it, and we've been stuck with it ever since.

Letters of Complaint   The best way to write a letter of complaint is to write two, one an absolute sizzler, describing in detail your correspondent's probable ancestry and habits, then another complimenting him profusely and taking all the blame yourself for whatever stupidity he committed. You throw the first letter away and mail the second.

The reason is this: You don't know precisely who in all that great big mail-order company sent you the size 18 puce-and-persimmon housedress instead of the bale of peat moss you ordered. Whoever opens your letter certainly didn't do it. All she does is open letters. But the sizzler—had you mailed it —might make her so mad that she'd bury it permanently under her lunch in her bottom desk drawer.

However, if your second letter is larded with mealy-mouthed phrases like "My printing may not have been clear," and "I'm sorry to mention this because your service has always been *so* satisfactory," and so on, you may eventually get your peat moss.

A CHILD'S GARDEN OF COMPLIMENTARY CLOSES

affectionately	best wishes	love
all the best	cordially	lovingly
always	devotedly	ruefully, etc.
as ever	ever	sincerely
best regards	faithfully	your
best to you	fondly	yours

The complimentary close can be uncomplimentary, unless you evaluate your relationship precisely as your correspondent does. Send out a *lovingly* and get back a *sincerely*, and you have a small wound to lick.

Which you use is a matter of preference and habit. Personally, I find *cordially* condescending. *Best regards* means little, unless I know my correspondent has second-best ones too, for his second-best friends. *Affectionately* seems to me to meter the warmth; *lovingly* is a bit lavender-and-smelling-salts; *your* and *yours* mean nothing or everything; *faithfully* is cold; *always* leaves the question "always what?" *Devotedly*— a favorite with the etiquette books—is good if you think in italics and say things like "the most idiotically marvelous pie-crust." But it doesn't fit any relationship of mine, unless I were writing a love letter, and if I were, I should think I could do better than that. I know a man who signs his letters *relentlessly*.

Of course, you needn't use a complimentary close at all. It's more interesting and equally friendly to tuck a bouquet or two into the body of the letter. "I've thought of you so much lately. . . ." or "How I wish I could see you!" Then you can end with something casual like "I must run now—the palomino's foaling! Jane." (These breezy endings aren't too easy to think up, but anything worth-while takes doing. If you want to buy a pregnant palomino and use this one, you may.)

The Calling Card Calling cards are the small rectangular affairs engraved with your name that are home in the desk drawer when you're out shopping and need one to enclose with a gift. This is infuriating, because you must then use the plain card provided by the shop, and no one ever discovers that you own any engraved calling cards at all. The remedy is to take a stack into the village some day and leave them wherever you customarily buy gifts: the bookstore, the florist, the little Danish gift shoppe. They'll keep them for you somewhere in a marked envelope. Then, if you buy enough gifts, *many* people will know you have engraved calling cards. Furthermore, you'll get credit for choosing the gift in person, when all you probably did was to telephone.

Hardly anyone—except for military or diplomatic personnel and people over ninety—uses calling cards to call with today, because it's rude to drop in at any house that has a telephone (see page 12). And if you *did* drop in, the hostess would probably answer the door herself. Calling with calling cards implies the presence of butlers or maids and silver card trays, all of which are getting scarce.

Calling cards make good bookmarks, too. They seem to hold up better than little pieces torn from a newspaper.

Or you can use them in birth announcements. This is a good way to get rid of a lot of cards at once. You have tiny cards made for the new baby—no Master or Miss, just the name— and the stationer attaches them to *your* cards, umbilical style, with blue or pink ribbon. (This may seem pretty cute, but you could do worse, and many people have. A magazine once held a contest for Cleverest Birth Announcements. If memory serves, and I am afraid it does, a lift-truck engineer and his wife announced their New 1962 Model, Hydraulically Equipped, Loud Horn, a television family announced a Late Late Show— it was a ten-month baby—and a photographer announced a Little Snapshot, 9 Months Developing.)

You can, of course, use calling cards as invitations. Write

Cocktails 5:30-7:30
R.s.v.p.

If you know the people well, cross out your engraved formal name and write your first name or names in by hand (see page 16).

This really hasn't many advantages. The Post Office says you can't mail that tiny card in its own envelope, so you must drop it into a bigger one. Also, a brusque invitation like this can seem rude, somehow. Like yelling FOOD! to a starving man, it seems to imply that your friends will come running at the sniff of a wet cork. Still, you know your friends better than I do, and if it's all right with them, it's certainly all right with me.

Business Letters   The prime rule with business letters—as opposed to personal letters—is to answer them promptly. This helps you stay in business, if you are, and if you're not, it keeps your desk top clearer.

This section will be brief, because business letters have improved immensely since the days of "Yours of the 17th inst. at hand and in reply would state . . ." Business courses and schools are sweeping the gobbledygook right out, most business firms have their own sensible style sheets, and I can think of only a few matters that need clarifying.

One is the matter of names.

No female should sign a business letter with her initials only: J. B. Cotter. In the past, this has not only confused people, it has inspired some of the worst magazine stories you ever read, in which J. B. Cotter turns out to be this perfectly gorgeous girl, and this very handsome young man keeps writing her these terribly insulting letters under the impression that she's a he, but finally . . . It's all right if she puts (Miss) in front of it. Or (Mrs. James B.)* underneath it. But she must do one of these things, for the sake of her correspondent.

And men should be careful. Any man with a sweet little name like Marion, Leslie, Cecil, or Lyle can quite properly put (Mr.) in front of it, and he'd better do so, lest he be emasculated in his correspondent's next letter.

By the way, one place where a woman can sensibly use her initials in masculine fashion is on her big-city apartment house mailbox and door, if she lives alone or with another woman. It can prevent her being bothered by men with curious ideas of etiquette. This has nothing to do with writing letters, but it is handy to know. And it's wise to use only her initials in the telephone book, for the same reason.

If you are important enough to have your name on the business letterhead, you can afford an illegible signature with no

---

* But preferably not (Mrs. Janet B.), whether she is a wife, widow, or divorcée. "Mrs." plus the given name belongs only on legal documents, not at the end of any social or business correspondence.

name typed beneath it. But if your name isn't on the letterhead, and you can't write, it must be typed, or your correspondent will be hamstrung when it comes to addressing you. He cannot write to Mr. Phlpppft.

This is a signature I received the other day from my bank. It is reproduced here in the faint hope that the man (woman?) who wrote it may one day see it, and step forward, and let me know what to call him.

Yours faithfully,

FOR MANAGER.

Another point to remember is not to make business letters too perfect. In this day of the electric typewriter, perfectly typed letters can look like printed forms. Some firms insist on one mistake per letter, corrected by pen—the print of the potter's thumb, the personal touch.

Writing to Someone You Don't Know   Some people are annoyed by letters from strangers beginning "Dear John Jones." In this day of ubiquitous first-naming, they consider it an invasion of privacy. Certainly there's little reason for "Dear John Jones," for it is always correct to call a man "Mr.," once he's reached the age of eighteen.

But with women it can make a certain sense, particularly women who use professional names. As a writer, I am often addressed by strangers who don't know my married name as "Dear Peg Bracken," which, though cozy, is at least correct. (I am not Miss Bracken, nor am I Mrs. Bracken, and I somehow don't care to be Madam.)

Consider this situation: If you write to the millinery firm of Suzi Reynolds & Mimi Peters—knowing nothing of their marital status—how will you address them? *Dear Ladies* is beyond the pale. *Mesdames* makes no more sense than would *Señoras*. *Dear Madams,* which the etiquette experts recommend, sounds perfectly awful. *Dear Suzi Reynolds and Mimi Peters*, it seems to me, is a sensible solution. And *Dear Sirs* would—oddly enough—be a sensible solution, too; for you can start any business letter to any plural-named firm, masculine or feminine, in that fashion.

Still, those aren't the most sensible solutions. Which brings us to one of the best business inventions since the coffee break.

The Simplified Business Letter   Since World War II, this has steadily gained converts, from both business offices and people writing *to* business offices, and no wonder. With the S.B.L. you can skip the faintly foolish "Dear Sirs" (sirs you've never met and never will), as well as the undeservedly stern "Gentlemen." And you needn't weigh the feather-light subtleties of "Yours very truly" and "Very truly yours." And you can even quit balancing and centering and indenting. For the S.B.L. dispenses with all salutations and complimentary closes, and the whole thing is flush on the left. It states its business and gets down to it. Like this:

August 21, 1963

Jeannette E. Hopkins
Harcourt, Brace & World, Inc.
757 Third Ave.
New York 17, New York

Missing manuscripts

You are right, Miss Hopkins. I thought the original
and one carbon of the manuscript had gone out to you
three Saturdays ago. However, I discovered them
yesterday afternoon, somewhat waterlogged, in my
daughter's bicycle basket.

Corrective measures have been taken on all fronts,
and the two copies boarded the 8:45 plane for New
York this morning.

I'm sorry about the delay.

Peg Bracken

Upson Downs
Portland 1, Oregon

III

✿

THE
SMALLER
ISSUES

". . . there is a certain stream of irritability that is continually fretting upon the wheels of life. . . ."
—WILLIAM HAZLITT

CHAPTER EIGHT

Some
Sticky Wickets

"Le silence éternel des espaces infinis m'effraie...."*
—PASCAL

This is an interesting thought, tidily expressed, and one can understand M. Pascal's feelings. Still, I doubt if he'd have found
much comfort in space today, either. The noisier it gets out

* Here, by the way, is an etiquette problem frequently encountered
by writers: To translate or not to translate? *After all* (mutters the
writer), *he said it in French, and a lot of people know French, and
I'd look pretty condescending if I translated, like "The silence of
infinite space scares me to death," now wouldn't I?* The writer says
all this to himself, knowing full well that the real reason he included
it was that a little French really jazzes up the look of a page. So he
puts in the translation and takes it out and puts it in. . . . Nothing
is easy.

there, the more inscrutable and enormous our problems seem to become.

It is a relief, therefore, to turn to some small scrutable problems, BB-shot size, which can be either solved, rationalized away, or simply skipped:

- forgetting names, and that sort of thing
- unintentional rudeness and discomforts
- impossible questions and some possible answers
- the *faux pas*

All these things may make for a choppy chapter, but remember, we are paddling in choppy seas.

Names and Introductions   A big trouble here is that people are too slow to help each other out. Someone—whose name is at the tip of your tongue and stays there—simply stands, waiting to be introduced. Only when the gathering silence is thick enough to walk a mouse across does he tell the people what to call him. (And sometimes he never does. In this case, all you can do is mutter, "Of course, I know you, but I simply can't remember your name," or "Introduce yourselves, please, I'm dim today"—neither of which covers you with any glory.)

The fact is, everyone owes it to everyone to announce his own name whenever he may have to be introduced—otherwise, that long muddy silence is all his fault. And he'd better announce it even if his own mother is in the group. Mothers can draw some remarkable blanks, too.

Also—for purposes of general ease—when he meets someone out of context, he can remember that he's out of context, himself. Like the dry cleaner. He is easy to recognize behind his dry-cleaning counter because you *expect* to see him there, but not at the next table in the Coffee Shop. And he is probably having the same problem with you. So, here again, names help.

Furthermore, husbands and wives must co-operate. When a woman, in the company of a female friend, meets her own husband, she must sound out her friend's name loud and clear, thus cueing her husband in. To many husbands, their wives' female friends all look alike, no matter how many times they see them.

Men should be similarly helpful when they are together and one of their wives happens along. Many a man mistakenly thinks his wife should be able to distinguish Paul Beaver from

Peter Chipmunk—and them in their gray flannel suits, too—just because she sees them once a year at the office party.

Never mind if you can't remember the names of new acquaintances, especially when you're meeting many people at once. This parlor trick is hardly worth learning, for it usually makes people suspicious. The person who can do it has to *prove* he can, and, accordingly, he uses your name too often. "I agree with you, Mrs. Carrington-Smithers," he says, "but on the other hand, Mrs. Carrington-Smithers, did it ever occur to you that . . ." What *does* occur to you is that he's going to put you on a mailing list or try to sell you something. You wouldn't trust him an inch.

Sometimes, to be sure, one wants to pretend one is brighter than one is. Say you've been chatting at length with a new acquaintance, whose name you've already forgotten or never heard in the first place, when you sense danger to windward. You're going to have to introduce him. You can do this:

Interrupt yourself or your acquaintance to ask, with a good show of scientific interest, "Incidentally, just how *do* you spell your name?" If he answers, "P-H-L-E-U-G-E-L," your façade is intact. But if he says, surprised, "Why, W-I-L-S-O-N," you must know how to handle yourself. In this case you nod thoughtfully and say, "That's what I figured. Funny thing, though—I've a friend named Wilson, but he spells it with *two* L's. W-I-L-L-S-O-N." Actually, there's hardly a name that can't be spelled several ways. You can usually think of some variation, which may lead to some dreary talk about names in general, but at least you've got your foot out of the bucket.

When you know you've been introduced to someone before, but he seems unaware of it, it's best to say a pleasant, noncommittal "How do you do." (If you say, "Oh, but we've *met!*" it might flatter him because you remembered, while embarrassing him because he forgot.)

Still, there are limits. Some people, either absent-minded or nearsighted,* can meet you time and again without remembering it, which presently becomes infuriating. I feel, myself, that such rudeness can be justifiably countered with a flat-footed

---

* It's true that you sometimes look better to other people without your glasses on, and they look better to you, too, when you eventually see them. But a simple case of myopia can cause wounded feelings, which contact lenses could probably prevent, if you hate your glasses all that much.

clarification of the issues at hand. Once, on being introduced for the fourth time in five weeks to the same woman, I did this:

"Look at me," I said. "Find some identifying trade-marks. I wear my hair like this, you see. My ears are pierced, and I usually wear gold button earrings. My name is—" and I pronounced it with great clarity. "I'm pointing all this out," I said, "in the hope that we'll never have to be introduced again." And we never were.

If you can help it, don't introduce anyone as a relative of a rather well-known person. Saying "Mrs. Caraway, the astronaut's sister" makes her feel that that's the only reason she was invited, which it probably is, but there's no sense stressing it. The fact that she is the astronaut's sister is bound to leak out.

And one other point, more pertinent to etiquette than you might think, is this: It's unwise to introduce two good friends of yours with the "You two will get along like a house afire!" approach. This saddles them with the embarrassingly awkward responsibility of loving each other immediately. And they probably won't, for, as Santayana has said, "Friendship is almost always the union of a part of one mind with a part of another; people are friends in spots." Just because your own spots are compatible with some of the spots of your two friends doesn't mean that theirs will necessarily meld with each other's.

What to Call Clergymen   This is quite simple in spite of the millions of words the big fat etiquette books devote to it. After all, you're not expected to know the various gradations of rank and the other complexities of all the organized and unorganized religions. You know what you need to know about addressing the clergy of your own church (and if you don't, you may certainly ask the head of it or the church secretary). Otherwise, knowing these points will take care of most situations:

You call a Jewish clergyman "Rabbi Rosen." Or just plain "Rabbi" (for "rabbi" means master or teacher, and the word can stand alone). You call a Catholic clergyman "Father Brown." Or just plain "Father." (The word "Father" too, can stand alone.) You call a Protestant clergyman "Mr. Jones," unless you are sure he has a doctorate,* in which case you call

---

* But it's best not to call anyone "Dr." unless you're fairly positive he is. If he isn't, he'll be embarrassed and feel duty bound to correct you. Whereas, the other way around, he will take a modest pride in upping the "Mr." to "Dr.," and no harm will have been done.

him "Dr. Jones." (You can't call him "Reverend" as a noun—
"I want you to meet the Reverend"—because "reverend" is an
adjective, which can*not* stand alone; it would be like saying,
"I want you to meet the dark-haired." But you can speak
of him, of course, as "the Reverend Mr. Jones."

In writing letters to them, you follow the same forms: Rabbi
Stephen Rosen—Dear Rabbi Rosen. Father Anthony Brown—
Dear Father Brown. The Reverend John Jones—Dear Mr.
Jones.

About Shaking Hands   Technically, women call the shots here.
Some women are natural-born handshakers, some aren't.
(European women shake hands more often than do American
women.) If a woman wants to, she extends her hand. But if a
man beats her to it, she must shake hands with him unless she
wants to make it clear that she doesn't like him. In actual practice, of course, it doesn't matter a whit who gets there first. And
both sexes may properly shake hands with gloves on, and no
apologies.

It is a pleasantly cordial gesture for a hostess to shake hands
with each arriving guest. Shaking hands is also a good way
of getting your guests to go home (see page 24).

And now for some of the small unintentional rudenesses and
discomforts—the sand in the daily machinery, and quite as
plentiful as the sands on the beach.

Consider, for instance, the laddie who strides to the elevator
where you and a number of others have been waiting, and
forcefully pushes the button. He shouldn't have done it. He
should have credited you and the rest with the rudimentary
brain needed to push it for yourselves.

Or this: Looking your 10:00 A.M. loveliest, at the grocer's,
you've been having a dreary old fight with the clerk over the
price of the dog food. When an acquaintance bumps your
elbow and beams, "I've been watching you for hours!" you
want to hit her. There are times when you prefer to be invisible,
that's all. Your veneer is temporarily mislaid and you can't
think where you put it. Other people should sense these times
and not see you.

"Aren't You So-and-So?"   It is poor social policy to ask of a
vaguely familiar face, "Aren't you So-and-So?" or "Don't you
work for Such-and-Such?" This often happens to me, for I

seem to resemble a lot of other people, and it's always depressing.

Last time was in a downtown drugstore. The clerk, who stared at me hard, finally asked, "Don't you work in the barbershop across the street?" I assured him I didn't. "Didn't you ever work there?" he persisted. "No," I said, truthfully. Out of curiosity, then, I walked across the street to see what their beat-up old manicurist looked like. But they had no manicurist, only a lady sweeping out.

The Language of the Flowers Flowers can say many pretty things: "Welcome back," or "Have a marvelous time," or "Stay with it, we're rooting for you," or "I love you."

But the language of the Corsage is different. A couple of gardenias means that he hasn't much money or imagination, one or the other and possibly both. And a corsage of baby orchids or adult orchids or anything else, usually bedreadfuled with shiny ribbon, usually means that the man, or the organization, or the committee wanted to make a gracious gesture but didn't quite think it through.

Indeed, the corsage is a truly sticky wicket, which it is time to unstick.

Facts must be faced: Most women, dressing for a special occasion, plan their costumes carefully from earrings to shoes, keeping always in mind what a mother-in-law of mine called the toot ensemble of the whole. For fouling this up, nothing is so effective as a last-minute corsage, chosen by the Program Chairman, who just loves pink rosebuds.

And our friend—if she has any manners—can't refuse it. She must bite the bullet and pin the rosebuds onto her gold wool suit, probably obscuring her new, carefully chosen, chunky gold clip—but a gallant lady to the end. (However, if she'd brought along a small fabric bag instead of a leather pocketbook, she could properly have pinned them to that, and with less pain. This is a good thing to remember in any corsage-prone situation.)

The corsage rule, then, is this: Find out if she likes to wear them, or whether they make her feel like a moose. If she *does* like to wear them, ask her what kind she would like. And if she says she does *not* enjoy wearing a corsage, and if you're an organization, not just a man, put the money into the club fund for crippled children. Or give her a similarly priced but more or less permanent momento. No one objects to a superlative linen handkerchief. (If she is wholly of the Kleenex persuasion, she'll still appreciate it, for she can give it to someone else for Christmas.)

One more random item comes to hand, this one concerning snapshots, photographs, and what to say about them

You can't tell, and often you wouldn't believe, how someone else hopes he looks. Therefore, it is unwise to say, "What a perfect likeness!" even though it's so flattering you wouldn't recognize it. Also, the more dazzling it is, the more important it becomes not to ask, "How long ago was this taken?" Your safest reaction is a ruminative "Wellll . . . it doesn't exactly flatter you, but I suppose it's a record of the occasion."

"May I borrow your comb? I have this awful scalp disease and I hate to use mine."   —PHYLLIS DILLER

Some questions are simply unanswerable.

For example, a woman I know—forced to renege at 6:00 P.M. from a dinner I was giving for her and her husband —said several times, "And I'll bet you went to a lot of trouble! *Did* you go to a lot of trouble?" I didn't want to make her feel worse by saying I'd gone the whole route and dragged out the party hats and the nut cups. Still, I didn't want her to think I hadn't even dusted off the table.

Have you stopped beating your wife?

Then there are the too-personal questions.

For instance, about children. Some couples with children regard the lives of childless couples as being pointless and empty. They are, unfortunately, prone to ask, "Why don't you have any?" Now, there are, of course, many possible reasons— physiological, financial, professional, and just plain personal. (Some childless couples regard the lives of childful couples as being dull beyond belief, bounded on three sides by Pablum, plastic pants, and Winnie-the-Pooh, and on the south by Disneyland.)

But childless people are more polite and don't say these things, nor do they ask questions like "Why in the world did you bother to produce a little creature like that?" which would be just as courteous.

The whole subject is best steered clear of.

"May I ask what a company like Amalgamated Widget pays a man in your husband's position?"

"Yes indeed! Ask all you like."

"I'm curious—what *did* that water color cost?"

"Twice as much as it's worth."

You may, of course, be blunt, and say, "I'm sorry, but I can't answer that question."

You may say, "I haven't the faintest idea."

You may say, "If you'll forgive my not answering that question, I'll forgive your asking it." (This usually wilts the hardiest question-asker. Oddly enough, it is kinder to say cheerfully, "None of your damn business," if this fits in with your personal vernacular.)

Just as some questions can't or needn't be answered, some shouldn't be asked.

When something devastating has happened to a friend, it's important to remember that you don't know about it (even though you've heard about it on the grapevine) until your friend tells you. Because maybe you're an island in the sun to your friend, a chance for him to pretend it never happened.

(It is different when the bad thing happened to the relative or friend of a friend. But even here, one must use one's head. If your friend's uncle is in the hospital with double pneumonia, ask. If he is in a drying-out place, don't.)

Or take the case of the returned traveler. When he finally telephones you with a "Here I am home again, little old adventurous Me!" don't ask "When did you get back?" This can make him feel obscurely guilty that he didn't call sooner. Maybe it's taken him three weeks to get organized.

Also, when someone telephones you with an "I tried to get you yesterday," don't ask "When?" even though you were at home all day, with your telephone in good working order. People just *say* these things, you know, and there's no point pasting them to the mat. A vague "I *have* been hard to find lately" is kinder.

One other point: Because good manners involve not forcing other people to abandon theirs, it's best not to ask a female acquaintance for a recipe, or the name of her perfume, or her sources of supply— "*Where* did you find that wallpaper? I want some just like it." Many women consider these things to be trade secrets. Of course, you can whoop, "What a perfectly marvelous fresh *fresh* scent!" and if the lady isn't totally thick-headed (which she can't be or she couldn't have picked such a pretty smell in the first place) she will recognize this for the Hint Unmistakable, which it is. Then she can either pick it up or leave it alone.

PLEASE DON'T EAT THE DOILIES

So we come, by a fairly logical route, to the *faux pas,* or dropped brick. Here we'll draw a clear line between this, which rocks someone else's boat, too, and the so-called embarrassing moment, which usually rocks only your own.

For instance, when Senator and Mrs. Philander Knox were entertaining the Chinese ambassador at a formal dinner, about forty years ago, finger bowls were passed during the last course. The ambassador removed his glass bowl all right, but didn't notice the sheer lace doily beneath it. Then, when a molded ice was passed, he put it on top of the doily and later was seen to spoon the whole works into his mouth—ice cream and doily, too.

This could have been embarrassing to the ambassador, had he not been able to swallow it (although he was). And it was a distressing moment for his hostess, although you'd think she might have whispered, "Forgive me for not warning you—just spit it into your napkin and no one will notice."

Still, it was merely a mildly unfortunate occurrence—certainly not a *faux pas,* for no one's feelings were wounded.

> ". . . [*the Duke of Edinburgh*] *has cultivated the art of what he calls 'dontopedalogy'—opening his mouth and putting his foot in it.*"   —ANTHONY SAMPSON

One helpful preventative of the verbal *faux pas*—and most of them are verbal—is to keep a kind, uncritical tongue in the mouth when rowing in strange waters.

For instance, never inquire about someone—say, at a party —in other than complimentary or noncommittal terms. It is far better to ask, "Who is the interesting woman in the sequins?" than "Who's the 1926 belle with the false teeth?" for the gentleman you're asking is undoubtedly her husband.

And one must beware of making dogmatic statements that

allow of no loopholes. Take the case of the Bronzed Baby Shoes.

A decor-minded friend of mine was dining with her husband at the home of some new friends. When the talk turned to matters of good taste, my friend said, with emphasis, that its true nadir was bronzed baby shoes. And as she said it, she saw —but too late to stop saying it—a pair of them on the mantel.

A few months later, when the couple dined at another house, and no wonder, the husband was regaling the guests with the incident. Finishing his story, he glanced for the first time at the top of the grand piano, and—you guessed it. There they were.

It's an interesting point that in situations of this sort the brickdropper can do little, other than ooze into the middle distance and wish he were dead. Unfairly enough, reparations are up to the droppee, who must hold firmly in mind that no matter how bruised his own feelings are, the brick-dropper feels worse. First aid must be rushed to him immediately: loud cheerful laughter, change of subject, change of scene—whatever comes to mind. In the above instance, it was up to the hostess to chuckle merrily, while her heart bled for her baby shoes. "Yes, aren't they the *end!*" she can say. "They were Aunt Winifred's idea, and you know Aunt Winifred. . . ."

Life is sometimes very hard.

CHAPTER NINE

Penny Ante with
Auntie Penny

The question-and-answer technique has long held an honorable place in the etiquette business. To help make this book truly representative, then, let's let Auntie Penny have her say.

Dear Auntie Penny,

   I'm being married pretty soon, thank goodness, but I sort of have this feeling more or less that I shouldn't exactly wear a white wedding dress if you know what I mean. Do you think I can wear a white wedding dress?

                                    STOOPED TO FOLLY

Dear Stooped:

Well, this more or less depends on several factors, in a manner of speaking. What I mean is, if white actually meant today what white used to be supposed to mean, if you follow me (although if it always did, how did Grandma learn to count so fast on her fingers?), they wouldn't be selling all the white wedding dresses today that they're selling. Or, to put it another way, white is perfectly all right, depending on the grapevine and the waistline. Good luck!

Dear Auntie Penny,

There is a member of our bridge club I'd like to know better, but I don't know if she'd like to know me better, because she is quite interesting but I am not very. How can I tell whether to invite her to lunch some time? I am not tactful or subtle or anything, I am just a

SIMPLE HEART

Dear Simple:

When you study tactful, subtle people (and believe me, Auntie's been at it for years), you find that they usually talk *fast* and bury things *in the middle*. It involves some babbling. For instance, you'd go about the lunch business like this: ". . . and so I was driving out there past the Red Mill— by the way, it might be fun to have lunch there some time—and it started to rain; why, I never saw such a downpour. . . ."

That way, you see, the Interesting Lady can pick it up or not, and you're not just standing there twisting your sash.

Dear Auntie Penny,

My husband and I always go to football games with five other couples. We meet in the Club Lounge beforehand and always one fellow insists on paying for the whole first round of drinks. So then the next fellow has to prove what a big wheel *he* is, and if a wife objects, she looks chintzy, but there goes the next payment on the freezer, and what are you going to do?

BURNED UP & BROKE

Dear Burned:

Nothing, except get there thirty seconds before the kickoff. Because when the other lads pound their chests, your boy will also have to pound his, for this is the law of the jungle. They couldn't solve Skybolt, either.

Dear Auntie Penny,

My husband's daily office grind make him tired and crabby, and every weekend his gardening makes him tired and crabby. So we hardly ever go out because he is too tired and crabby, and our social life is Nowheresville. What shall I do? I've had it.

UP TO HERE

Dear Up:

No, you haven't had it, you're just getting it. This not-unusual behavior pattern is known among psychiatrists as Party-poopers' Syndrome. *But your husband can be cured!* What he probably needs is a

SWIFT KICK

Put 1½ ounces cognac in a glass. Wrap a thin lemon slice around a cube of cocktail sugar (or around ½ teaspoon plain granulated sugar). Dip this into the cognac and eat half of it, rind and all. Then drink *all* the cognac, right down. Then eat the other half of the lemon slice.

This is a drink from the old prize-fighter days with remarkable restorative powers for people with that knocked-out feeling. Give him one the minute he comes in, if you're going out that night. Give him two, if he insists, and he'll carry you piggyback down Main Street.

Dear Auntie Penny,

Do you have to telephone thanks for a lunch? Tea? Cocktails? Dinner? I've noticed that some people do and some don't, and I'm just

WONDERING

Dear Wondering:

That's quite a can of beans you just opened. But let's consider it, bean by bean.

First, look into the local drill; it's different in different locales. If you can't find out, here's the general rule: Plain vocal thanks at the door are plenty for lunch, tea, or cocktails (unless the affair was given for you, in which case you send a note the next day, and flowers or some other thoughtful little gift*).

---

* For instance, if the place was pretty clean, a copy of *The I Hate to Housekeep Book,* by Peg Bracken, Harcourt, Brace & World, Inc., 1962.

After a dinner, the rule says, telephone the next day or write a note. But if you ask Auntie Penny, and I think you just did, scratch the phone call and write the note. Your hostess is up to her neck the next day stuffing the Sèvres back into the break-front and getting the kids to the dentist's, and she's fresh out of the old social vim.

And notes are quicker. Just say, "We had a lovely time—thanks again, so much!" (Once I got one that said

"Your party was delightful,
I'm feeling simply frightful!"

and this was okay with Auntie Penny, too.)

Dear Auntie Penny,
    Last night my husband and I went to a bride's first dinner and there weren't any napkins. My husband said I should ask for them, but I said No, it might hurt her feelings, so I didn't. Who was right?

GREASY ALL OVER

Dear Greasy:
    Well, Greasy, he was. *Sure* she had napkins, and now maybe she's blushing because she thinks *you* think she didn't. You see, you can always ask for basics: knife, fork, spoon, salt, pepper, sugar, water, napkins. Cream for coffee is something else again, though. If you *want* coffee cream and there's none visible, you may say brightly, "Black coffee has such an *interesting* taste, doesn't it!" If she has some cream, then, she'll probably fetch it. Otherwise she can agree that it certainly does, and no harm done.

Dear Auntie Penny,
    We've got six kids and a big house, and my husband's mother was a spotless housekeeper; but when he comes home at night, the only thing that's shining is my nose. So then he gets mad and loses his manners and mine go to pot too. Can this marriage be saved?

OVERWORKED & UNDERPAID

Dear Overworked:
    Certainly! Just before he comes home, put a dab of furniture polish behind each ear, dear. Then, when he shows, give him a big sweet kiss.

Dear Auntie Penny,

What is the right wineglass for port? Are Burgundy glasses taller than Chablis glasses? Should you use those great big snifters or those middle-sized ones for brandy?

TERRIBLY NERVOUS

Dear Terribly:

Just calm down now, while Auntie Penny explains.

Once upon a time, an etiquette-book writer, whose Daddy owned a drinking-glass factory, started the rumor that you need a different glass for each wine: wee conical glasses for sherry, small bulbous glasses for port, tall-stemmed goblets for table wines, and so forth.

Well, her Daddy was delighted, because the rumor spread like measles. People started thinking they couldn't serve Chablis without Chablis glasses or Rhine wine without *Römer,* and Daddy started manufacturing all sorts of weird shapes and sizes, and now he has a lovely villa in Italy where he sits around drinking the *vino paesano* out of anything handy, the way the rest of the people do.

All you need is one kind of wineglass: a stemmed goblet that's narrower at the top than at the widest part of the bowl, and holds from seven to nine ounces. And you may correctly serve any kind of wine in it. If it's table wine, pour it two-thirds full; sherry or port, one-third full; brandy, a little less.

Then give your itty-bitty one-and-one-half-ounce sherry glasses and so on to the little bride down the street who doesn't know any better.

Dear Auntie Penny,

Yes, but what about champagne? In glasses like that you couldn't watch the pretty bubbles rise.

NOT QUITE SO NERVOUS NOW

Dear Not:

So *get* hollow-stemmed glasses if you are a bubble-fancier. But don't think you have to. There are purists who say you shouldn't drink champagne out of hollow-stemmed glasses anyway, because your fingers around the stem will warm the champagne.

So do it as you like it.

It is also permissible on honeymoons and so forth to drink champagne in bed out of a toothbrush glass, but be sure you remove the toothbrush first.

IV

❋

OUR
COMMON
PREDICAMENT

"In our disturbed and uncertain age, not knowing where we are going, how and if we shall get there, the least we can do is to treat one another with a certain amount of respect."
—ROMAIN GARY

CHAPTER TEN

Lord Chatterley's Mistress: Men & Women & What to Do About It

"Let it never be said that love is an indolent calling."
—OVID

The subject of men and women versus etiquette is absolutely fraught with sex, which is as it should be. It is a good thing from other standpoints, too, for the fact greatly simplifies the approach to this chapter.

1. Good etiquette, for a man, is whatever makes a woman feel more like a woman, without making her feel weak-minded.

2. Good etiquette, for a woman, is whatever makes a man

feel more like a man, without making him feel more harassed and put upon than he normally does anyway.

These are the touchstones, then, against which to test any puzzling point of intersexual etiquette, whether in the elevator* or in bed. For today, with each sex doing so many of the same things, and push buttons doing most of the rest, both men and women need occasional reminders as to which team they're on.

It has come to my attention that some people have, as a matter of fact, forgotten. That is, some men would rather act like women, and some women would rather act like men, which makes for a certain confusion. But several books have already been written about this, so I won't need to go into it. This chapter will concern itself only with the old-fashioned clearcut kind of people, of whom there are still many around. It will not concern itself, however, with the sex-appeal factor (except insofar as it comes as a happy side effect of observing Points 1 and 2).

Lady writers in particular are always advising other women on how to attract men: *Fourteen Ways to Up Your Sex Appeal.*† And it is a curious fact that these pieces are often read and followed even by women who don't *want* any more sex appeal—say, a woman who has so much already that she's in perpetual hot water, or a woman who privately considers the whole thing a great nuisance and doesn't really want to get to where all that sex appeal would probably lead her. Like a vegetarian going to a great deal of trouble to make friends with the butcher.

At any rate, before upsetting your applecart to do the things those articles recommend, it's wise to take a look at the men attracted to the lady writer who is touting her own wiles. Of course, you seldom get a chance to—although, just once, I did. I met a couple of the men this charm expert had attracted, herself, and I decided I'd sooner draw flies. So each to his own, and you never can tell.

* "An almost outmoded grace that still thrills me utterly is to have a man take his hat off in an elevator when I enter. It makes me feel feminine and cherished—makes me feel, and act, much nicer for at least half an hour."

—Kay Taylor

† I don't know what makes them think they're oracles. It's common knowledge that female writers always resemble either horses or birds, and their fingers are usually smudgy from changing typewriter ribbons.

Actually, the glorious fact is that everyone—flat-chested or bulbous, silent or talkative, rosy or sallow, tiny or tall—*everyone* appeals to someone, as a cursory glance at one's married friends will attest.

But who can make rules? Some men think sultry perfume is sex-appealing; others like a fresh soap-and-water smell, like a little child's clean hair. Some women find a male mustache fetching; some find it scratchy. Many people haven't the slightest idea what they want till they marry it, or till they don't marry it and wish that they had.

So let's get down to where the work is—right into the etiquette of going out together and being out together—before we go on to the matter of living together, around the house and in the bedroom. (Most etiquette books never get into the bedroom, but this one will, because, after all, a great deal of etiquette takes place there, or ought to.)

Before getting mired in some minor details (what woman actually cares much whether a man is on the outside or the inside of an ordinary suburban sidewalk?), we'll look at some basics: for one thing, the etiquette of the invitation proffered the female by the male.

Here you're apt to get some real sparklers: "Want to go anywhere tonight, hon?" Or, "Nothing special you want to do, is there?" These approaches don't make a woman feel womanly, they make her feel either apathetic or domineering. (Now *she'll* have to think of something.)

What she would vastly prefer is the approach of a high-school boy I know. He phones a girl and says, "I'm going to go see that western at the Paramount tonight. Want to come?" If she doesn't, fine. He'll call somebody else. This lad will go far.

Some men would counter my thesis here with "Yes, but she never wants to do what I want to do." But this probably isn't so. If he clearly and enthusiastically wants to do it enough, *she* usually will—that is, if they like each other, and if they don't, what are we talking about?

Anyway, many women would like men to fight harder for their rights. There's too much male docility around, these days, and it's taken a lot of fizz out of the battle between the sexes.

Take the matter of who is supposed to go first.

Well, *he* is. Nearly every time. Common sense says so, and so does present-day etiquette, although many men have Ladies

First so firmly wedged into their heads that they often hang back when they shouldn't.

Women *like* men to go first. After all, the farmer walking six feet ahead of his wife across the cow pasture showed native gallantry, even though she *was* carrying the cow. He was blazing a trail around ditches and other unpleasant things she might have stepped in. A woman doesn't mind doing a little toting, so long as he will pioneer.

(If you ever saw a well-meaning man trying to get a woman through a revolving door ahead of him without knocking her hat off and her teeth in, you saw a good example of misguided manners. *He* should have gone through first. Then she'd have followed, on his push.)

Look at some other instances: He goes up a *ladder* first, for reasons of delicacy and so he can give her an assist at the top. He gets into a *cab* first, so she needn't scoot across the wide back seat to make room for him. Scooting is easier for someone in trousers. He goes first down a *train corridor*, because it's going to take biceps to open those stubborn doors between the cars. If he has no biceps, this will develop them. He goes first down a *theater aisle* if there's no usher. (If there is, she goes first, close to the wandering pool of light from the usher's torch.) He goes first into a dark *night club*. (This could be a nasty *bistro*, and he'd better lead the way.) He goes first into a *restaurant*, if no maître d' is there to greet them. Masterfully he finds a table. He climbs into a *bus* or *streetcar* first, to help her up. He gets off first, to help her down—unless it's crowded and she's nearest the door, in which case she'll just have to keep her eyes open and her wits about her and *move*.

An exception is *escalators*. Here she should go first—and she usually does, automatically, because she's on a high lope for the Dress Sale on Three. But he's supposed to be behind, anyway, to catch her if she slips.

Finally, HE GETS OFF A CROWDED ELEVATOR FIRST IF HE'S NEAREST THE DOOR. Women prefer this to being squashed by his gallantly hanging back. He should just get out.

It's all quite simple, you see. He goes first whenever that's easier or safer for her. And all these little items are valuable reminders to each sex of *la belle différence* between them.

Sometimes a man finds it hard to play his proper role with aplomb or even with good will. I asked a worldly man I know what annoys him most in the area of women and etiquette. After considerable thought, he said, "The woman who takes me for a salaried doorman when I hold open the door for her in a public building." He thought some more. "And," he added, "the forty women right behind her who know a good thing when they see it."

Then, too, when a woman slams full tilt into a man and waits for him to apologize, or hogs the middle of the escalator step so no one can get around her, or forgets that her umbrella points are at the average male's eye level, or that her free-swinging ten-pound pocketbook is a first-class battering-ram— Well, she does her cause no good, for men find it hard to be gallant to a Sherman tank. But many men would enjoy being more courtly, if women would make it easier.

". . . Pleasant as they have been, my years in the United States would have been even more agreeable if American women had allowed me to kiss their hands. . . . Despite my frustration, I still regard the kissing of a woman's hand as one of those small courtesies necessary for the preservation of that essential margin between men and women, which makes them both, in different ways, superior to each other and, therefore, again in different ways, and on a higher level, truly equal."
—ROMAIN GARY

Which isn't to say that she should be an entirely fragile blossom. Take modern car doors. Automotive companies pay high-priced talent to design latches that open at the touch of a pinkie, and so Antoinette might as well use hers. Or, if that is just more than she can bring herself to do, a man may correctly reach across her to open it for her.

A great deal of trivia has crept into intersexual etiquette, and that's a fact. For instance a man—saith the etiquette book —mustn't walk between two women, except when the trio crosses a street. But if he's the only man they've got, why mustn't he? The Book says it's because he'd have to turn his face away from one of them, in speaking to the other. But this isn't so terrible. Maybe each of these ladies enjoys having a man beside her, and if he weren't, she'd feel like Orphan Annie. Did they ever look at it that way?

Also, a man isn't supposed to take a woman's arm, except when crossing the street. But if she is wearing spike heels, or if it is spring (or summer, autumn, or winter) and they are in love, he certainly may. That's what this book says.

"A now famous Hollywood actor reveals his lower white-collar origins every time he sits down. He pulls up his trousers to preserve the crease."   —VANCE PACKARD

Consider Men's Hatiquette. It's simple, but many words have been wasted on it. Actually, all that matters is that he make sure his hat* is off whenever there's a roof or ceiling overhead—except for long covered thoroughfares like public halls and terminals, and in the Jewish temple, and on special ceremonial or costumed occasions.

Elevators are a moot point. Taking off his hat is a gracious gesture. But in a close-packed elevator it can create more distress than joy if he must elbow people and knock *their* hats off in the process.

He never has to take his hat off in the street, unless the flag goes by or stops. Not when a lady goes by or stops. The merest flick of the brim will suffice. And if it's a raw day, practical intersexual etiquette demands that he keep it securely on. Should he catch cold in his sinuses, some woman will probably have to nurse him or put up with him, and thus he hasn't proved to be so gallant in the long run.

MEN AND WOMEN IN RESTAURANTS

". . . If men dine alone, ten men together, how they dress I really don't mind. I'm not there. But if a man takes me out to dinner, I like him to smell of a nice soap, to wear his best suit, maybe black tie, so that I can wear my nice little dress. I will know then he has kindness of heart, he has said to himself, 'I will make a little effort so that she can look her best.' "
—LOUISE DE VILMORIN

Her point is well taken. Then, there are a few things she should remember, as well, and I am sure she does.

For one, not to keep him waiting too long before they even start out, while she decides that her make-up base is too light or her stockings too, well, purplish or something, and changes them. In most fair-to-good restaurants these days you need a miner's cap to read the menu by, anyway. Ten gets you twenty the man you're with won't notice what color stockings you're

---

* This goes for the convention hats with the funny tassels, too. Sometimes the boys forget, and keep them on in restaurants.

wearing, if any, but he'll certainly notice the three cigarettes he had time to smoke while he waited.

She should carry the minimum equipment. If she knows she'll need a complete valve-and-ring job by midevening, it's simpler to bring along a veil. I know a girl who tapes a lipstick, a dime, and a folded dollar bill above her knee (she could slip them into her bra, too) before she goes dining and dancing. This makes great sense—no swollen velvet pouch to end up in a man's pocket and make him heavy on his feet, or hers. (Of course, a girl must carry a small bag if she is lost without compact, cigarettes, and so forth. But it should have a wrist strap or loop, so she can wear it while she dances.)

As for mad money, which you don't hear much about these days, a charge account at a cab company can be handy. If this is a no-host evening, she won't need much money along, either. Sonia Goodkid always hands Bill Youngenbroke her contribution before they leave. Or if it is entirely her celebration, she'll have stopped in earlier and arranged with the restaurant to bill her later. (However, she'd better watch her step with this routine, or Bill will get the habit, and first thing you know, she'll be putting him through Med School.)

A working girl, any age and any job, pays for her own lunch when she lunches with a man. Or, at any rate, she is expected to, unless this is a budding office romance (which most wives will assume it is, if their spouses' lunch money starts disappearing with twice its usual feverish rapidity). She can give him a few dollars before they go into the restaurant—for her share of the bill—and hope she gets her change back. Or, if she knows he isn't sensitive about these things—and there's no reason he should be, at a business lunch—she can simply pay her own check and leave her own tip. Either way.

By the way, these financial matters should always be clearly understood all around, whether the situation is business or social. A woman I know gave a lavish restaurant party for three couples—she had been visiting in the city and this was the only way she could return their royal hospitality. The champagne flowed; she urged upon them the pressed duckling, the crêpes after the fashion of Suzette, the brandy; and her guests needed little urging. Finally, when she asked for her check, it developed that one of the gentlemen had already paid it. She protested, but he was adamant. All she could do was send him a note and a gift—a desk clock, it was. He owned two already, and she still feels indebted to her friends.

The worst female restaurant menace, according to men, is the woman who stops to chat—standing—with acquaintances at another table. A man feels ungentlemanly if he doesn't rise, and uncomfortable if he can't sit down immediately thereafter. A sweet smile from the lady, and a brisk hello, are sufficient, before she strides on. If she *has* to say something, she can send a note by the waiter.

Finally, to the matter of ordering. This is a male prerogative. Giving the order to the waiter will—back to our original touchstone—somewhat build the male ego, if he is knowledgeable about these things, and cares. But not if he isn't and doesn't. He'll properly consider it not worth the effort, if the menu is abstruse, or if the lady shuffles nervously from Crab Thermidor to Lamb Chops, with a short but dramatic pause at the Curry Indienne along the way. If she can't see her way clear, or if she wants to discuss sauces with the waiter, she'd better do her own ordering.

If there are more than two people at the table, each had better order. The host usually can't remember all that. Like a wrap-around skirt in a high wind, the whole thing is apt to blow up.

And so to a few rough notes on the Social Gathering, as it concerns men and women, and etiquette.

It is true that a man gets gold stars on a lady's ledger—which cancel some of the black marks on his rap sheet—when he tells her how pretty she looks (or handsome or well put together, as the case may be) before they go to a party, or while they're en route. But he gets double credit for telling her once they get there, for then it has twice the impact. The reason is this: Before she leaves home, a woman is tolerably satisfied with how she looks (or she wouldn't have left). Indeed, she is often delighted with her appearance—the naked black basic, the company face—wholly different from the rather soul-shattering reflection the mirror handed her early that morning. But once they arrive, her innocent glory is apt to be dimmed by all the *other* naked black basics and company faces, which in her excitement she had forgotten would be there. At this point, especially, she must know how she stacks up. *This* is the time to tell her.

Still, this is a minor point. A major one—or, to put it another way, what makes women the maddest—is the male tendency to herd together, drinking and talking shop. Many a woman asks for it, with her crossfire chitchat about purely female concerns, which drives the men perforce into the tall timber where the bottle is. But many a woman who doesn't ask for it gets it, too, which can have unhappy repercussions. After all, she didn't put on her company face and her nice little dress just to swap tatting patterns with Irene and Thelma. She'll be glad to do it for a while, mind you, but not all night.

The fact is that the virtuous housewife—if she doesn't work outside the house—sees and talks to few males alone, except for the milkman and the little old codger in the Blanket Department twice a year at White Sales. And this party—she thought—would be a chance to shine a little, showing a few pretty facets that may have rusted a bit at the kitchen sink. If she doesn't get to—if, on the contrary, she goes home feeling like the little woman in the tight permanent, with a pocketful of tuna recipes—she'll feel like kicking the cat.

This sorry state of affairs, with the sexes getting no practice in attracting and interesting each other, is often reflected in a certain lackluster performance in the bedroom, particularly where our heroine is concerned. Nothing has come alive for her, including herself, though the moon shine ne'er so brightly over the cowshed.

It is therefore an important part of male etiquette to make a woman feel womanly. It doesn't make her feel so when a man asks—first crack out of the box—what her husband does. It makes her feel *wifely,* and there is a huge though subtle difference. It's no good, either, to ask immediately about her children. This only makes her feel like a mother, and the fact that she is one may be something she'd like, momentarily, to forget. She wants to be treated as an attractive woman and a person in her own right, that's all, who can talk about something besides the egg money and the neighbors—as many a woman can, this lively age. And though the approach may frighten her at first, she will probably respond nobly.

GOOD MANNERS AND SEX

"The annelid worm spends its youth and adolescence in maleness; at the zenith of maturity it switches to femaleness."
—ELISABETH MANN BORGESE

This kind of annelid turnabout clearly has advantages. By the end of its mixed-up lifetime, the annelid should have a good worm's-eye view of how it feels to be each, which is more than can be said of most people. But so far as I can see, the system leaves the mature females with only teen-agers to consort with—the young worms, that is, who have not yet crossed the line. Thus, the annelid situation, too, leaves something to be desired. In this world, nobody has it 100%.

Now, sex per se is as interesting as it is overemphasized in the public prints, in this how-to age of hopefully easy specifics. The overemphasis is too bad, because it tends to make people think that their sex lives are what is the matter with them. If someone's is dull or nonexistent, he's apt to figure hopefully that a change of pace, or face, will put everything to rights, though it seldom works out that way.

It was some Stone Age man, I believe, who invented the myth that women are naturally monogamous, while men are not. Thus men were enabled to get double credit for cleaving to their marriage vows, while women were doubly damned if they didn't. And so things have gone, to the present day. If Grandfather's eye for a pretty ankle led him occasionally into greener pastures, he is fondly regarded as a picturesque old goat. But if Grandmother picked a few marigolds along the way, a discreet silence is maintained by all. And men still operate on a more elastic tether than do women, who have more to lose and who are not so free, in the nature of things, to do something about it.

"Some take a lover, some take drams or prayers . . ."
        —LORD BYRON

But drams or prayers are upsetting, to excess, and taking a lover is seldom satisfactory. For one thing, its practical aspects are difficult, because most communities frown on it. Indeed, nearly everyone disapproves, usually including the lady herself, for it may be against her marriage vows, or the way she was raised. Presently she may start wondering if it was only a pinch in the pass pantry, after all, and if she decides that it was, she may not like herself, which can be dangerous. Or things can go sour, which can be painful, although it only hurts when she breathes. And even though she clears these hurdles, others lie ahead. Perhaps she can't resist a natural female urge to turn a good lover into a bad husband, and presently there she is again, back at the same old stand.

On the whole, it is usually best, and saves an enormous amount of trouble, to work with the material at hand. With most of these puzzled people, if it weren't sex, it would be something else, for the ability to create and magnify one's own problems is one of our inalienable rights.

Most people need other things besides satisfactory sex in order to be reasonably happy—need to feel good and useful (because most people would *like* to behave themselves) and to know that they've helped to make other people happy or, at least, have done them no enduring harm. Additionally, nearly everyone needs to be warm, and fed, and healthy, and busy, and all that sort of thing.

Sex, therefore, isn't all the big deal that the past several decades would lead one to believe. It is, however, a splendid enterprise, albeit with comical overtones and aspects, not the least comical of which is one's mental picture of any humorless couple he knows, earnestly going about their homework with marriage manual in hand.

"Now you're supposed to pat me, George."

"I'm not so sure about that, Alma. It says right here, on page sixty-four . . ."

One worries about George and Alma, for they seem unaware of the fact that sex is as many-colored and personal as conversation—which was the word for it, a few centuries ago. *To converse* meant "to have commerce with a different sex," as Dr. Johnson delicately defined it in his dictionary, or, as we shall put it with equal delicacy, to make love. Certainly, the two activities have their similarities, especially in range of mood. Both can be ceremonial or merry, dutiful or impromptu, purposeful or absent-minded, passionate or tranquil, to name but a few. Both conversation and love-making are influenced by the frailest winds that blow. And what is good manners in each depends on the personalities and customs of the two people involved.

The manners of sex, therefore, is a foggy area. What the Joneses may consider perfect sex etiquette, the Johnsons might consider perfectly terrible. There are no absolutes.

Still, something can be said about timing.

"Venus herself is a mocking, mischievous spirit, far more elf than deity, and makes game of us. When all external circum-

stances are fittest for her service she will leave one or both the lovers totally indisposed for it." —C. S. LEWIS

Women, for the most part, want to make love when they feel loving. But often a woman doesn't make it clear that she does, and a man can't be blamed for becoming confused. Particularly when she greases her face at bedtime, wearing curlers with or without a pink grandma-type net bonnet that ties under the chin, and a bed bra (to keep her contours firm, as the advertisements say, but just what golden moment in the far future is she keeping them firm for?)—it's understandable if he reads or misreads all this as NO TRESPASSING. He may assume, naturally enough, that if the lady were willing, she would have made herself more generally beddable.

Also, if she breaks into his nesting murmurs with the fact that the washing machine broke down again, she can deflect him, whether she means to or not. Or if she insists on finishing a chapter, or seeing out the late, late show . . . For it is wise for a woman to remember that a man likes to make love when he feels loving, and at other times, too. When he feels like a conquering hero, for instance. And—just as often— when he doesn't feel like a conquering hero; when he feels, on the contrary, kicked around. This is constructive solace which she can offer.

It is infinitely good etiquette at these times for her to initiate the initiative and make *him* feel desirable. She may use the tactics of the skillful seducer, who leads the quarry to thinking along the proper or improper lines, then sits back quietly. Or she may go about it in any of a hundred ways, as Eve or Lilith dictates.

Then there are times, of course, regardless of physiological factors, when many a woman *is* reluctant about making love. We'll list them here. And if this seems to be a negative approach, nothing could be farther from the truth. Think of all the other times that are left.

1. *When she is feeling truly intense about a project.* And if he doesn't know what sort of thing she feels intense about, or when, he is in trouble already. Women feel intense about many things, from campaigns to club programs to begonia borders. Until she gets her project over the hump, he might as well watch television.

2. *When she is scrubbing the floor.* Or cleaning out the refrigerator, or occupied with any similarly dismal domestic

pursuit. She does not want the back of her neck kissed now. She does not appreciate the you're-always-beautiful-to-me-dear implication. She recognizes it for the cotton-pickin' lie that it is. It is important to wait until she feels dainty again, and charming.

3. *When she is making three dozen peanut-butter sand-wiches for the Cub Scouts, or engaged in another heavily maternal operation of this sort.* Now she is feeling harassed. Her mind is on motherhood and all the oatmeal responsibilities thereof, and she will be a hard girl to deflect. Furthermore, on the bottommost, unrecognized-but-nonetheless-there level of her subconscious, there is the awareness that she wouldn't be stuck with all those peanut-butter sandwiches in the first place, if it hadn't been for him.—Not a resentment, just an aware-ness. But at the moment, it is not operating in his favor.

4. *Right after she's used her lipstick brush.* Why did she spend nine whole minutes achieving that lovely clear lip line or otherwise applying a festive face? Not so he could mess it up immediately. It must be given a chance to mellow.

5. *After he's taken her to a foreign movie.* Husbands and wives often react differently to them. A man may drive home afterward with visions of sugarplums dancing through his head, and interesting notions of how *dolce la vita* can be. But it's best not to misinterpret the dreaming silence of the wife at his side. She may well be musing sourly on the high cost of getting to Rome and when, if ever, she'll be able to make it. Then, too, husbands are usually more gallant than wives are. Even though a wife would give Brigitte little or no serious competi-tion, her husband can generally close his eyes and pretend. But all that a wife can see, in her simple, childlike fashion, is that Lester just doesn't stack up so good, next to Horst or Mario or whoever. Lester had better give the impact a chance to wear off.

6. *After she has had a woeful evening* (see page 120).

7. *When she is just plain tired and sleepy.* On a vacation camping trip, say, after packing in, seven miles upcountry. If a man notices that she barely has the strength to open that can of meatballs, one romantic pass would be just one too many. He'd better give her a pat on the head and a kiss on the brow, saving the jollity for the early-morning hours when the birds are singing. He might start the coffee perking first, too, on the little gasoline stove.

8. *After she's returned from an unsuccessful clothes-shop-*

ping expedition. For many a wife, this is a traumatic experience. After looking at herself in a series of short tents under harsh fitting-room lights, she may be realizing she's not the girl she used to be, and probably never was. In fact, she can't imagine what her husband ever saw in her. It's best to wait for this little cloud to pass.

However, when she has found exactly what she was looking for, things are different. Now she has her healthy self-esteem back again and regards her lad highly, for having had the perception to pick her in the first place. Also, if he hasn't complained too much about the price—for whether it was her money or his, she's often aware of having diverted some family funds into luxury channels—she is *grateful.*

9. *At 8:00 Saturday morning for the 336th consecutive 8:00 Saturday morning.*

10. *After he has played the heavy father with the children (or she thinks he has).* No matter who was wrong or right, she will need time to cool off and warm up.

Indeed, sensible noises are far better than amorous advances, until any sort of a disagreement has been taken by the scruff of the neck and tidily settled. For—to repeat—most women prefer to make love when they feel *loving,* which is old-fashioned of them, but hardly culpable.

Which brings us to the etiquette of the heart, and to the gnat bites in any marriage—the thousand little ways in which men and women can and do annoy each other. For a thousand gnat bites can be mortal—if not to the marriage itself, to the physical side of it.

These things, too, are so personal that it is impossible to generalize. If only Alma wouldn't say *always* every time she corrects George ("Why do you *always* do thus and so?"), which multiplies his small transgression by two hundred. If George would—just once—notice her new dress with a "Say, that's pretty on you!" instead of a "How much did *that* set me back?" If only Alma would quit asking George why he can't fix a simple engine knock, when her dad could fix *anything.* If George would just once suggest that—inasmuch as *she* looked tired—*he'd* take the wastebaskets down to be emptied. . . .

But no outsider can ever say which tiny arrow reaches a vulnerable target, to the eventual detriment of the love-making, and which bounces merrily off the armor. It could be said that no man who calls his wife "Mother" and "Fats" all day can justifiably expect a bonfire that night—or, as Henry Fielding put it, "a warm partaker of the genial bed." Yet I know a man who has done this for 40 years, and with no ill effects whatsoever.

The only people who know are the two people immediately involved. They know, too, when their stockpile of mutual discourtesies has finally turned their physical life into a conversation in which nothing worth saying is said.

The popular experts pretend there are easy solutions (and such funny little solutions they think of!): "Fix your hair a becoming new way!"; "Major in fluffy nighties!"; "Tell him every day that you love him!"

But he probably won't notice the new Riviera bang, if so much boredom has set in, any more than she'll notice that he got a haircut. And he may only wonder, sourly, why she spent all that money for a new nightgown (997 out of 1,000 men prefer women without nightgowns anyway*—these figures from an unpublished and unmade survey which I'm going to make, the minute I have a minute).

As for telling him every day that she loves him, I know a woman who does this—while her minuscule warfare continues to prove otherwise—and her husband wears a hunted look.

Effective sex springs from deeper wells than these. And a renascence usually involves not only some agonizing self-appraisal but possibly scratching a dimension or two of the personality and developing a couple of others, which takes awareness, patience, faith, and work. No wonder the popular experts so seldom mention it.

But it is also true that remembering the small daily gallantries—which, as we've noted, help differentiate the sexes—helps subtly to make their physical relationship mean more than desultory conversation at a bus stop. For these courtesies contribute to self-esteem and to mutual esteem—both important ingredients in loving someone, in bed or, indeed, anywhere else.

* A 13th-century list of wifely vows includes an undertaking not to sleep in a chemise without her husband's consent.

CHAPTER ELEVEN

Raising the Child and
Lowering the Boom

"Do I look pretty, Mommy?"
"You look very nice, dear."
"But do I look pretty, Mommy?"
"Stop thinking about how you look, dear. You look very nice."

When you consider what some children go through, it's a wonder their mothers live to celebrate many Mother's Days; and when you consider what some mothers go through, it is a wonder they care to.

Today, the pitched battle between parent and child is nearly even-Steven. Each has a well-equipped arsenal. Also, each blushes for each in almost equal proportions. Parents often embarrass the living daylights out of their children, and vice-versa.

Here again, as in other areas, etiquette gets terribly mixed up with ethics. It is a parent's* bounden duty to teach a child rudimentary manners so he won't grow up too objectionable. It is a child's bounden duty not to make raising him any harder than it has to be. Not that these words will influence him. They are here only for the record.

Now, parents often forget their own rudimentary manners in dealing with children.

Take the little girl who started this chapter. Of *course* she looked pretty. Any little girl with the usual number of features arranged in the usual order looks pretty; and her parents had just better get this fact across to her so she can put it in its proper drawer and forget about it. Otherwise, there's no telling what back seats of how many hot rods she may find herself in —at an astonishingly early age, too—trying to prove her appeal. So this little girl's mother was breaking a signal rule of etiquette (had her neighbor asked hopefully if she liked her new suit, of course she'd have said Yes) as well as laying a good base for possible future ethical problems.

In the main, only *small*-children-and-etiquette will be discussed here, for once the primary building blocks are in place, it's to be hoped that children will absorb the good manners around them as they grow, with a short time out for being teen-agers.

Of course, parents can *try* to do something about teen-agers. They can try to explain that youth and charm are not necessarily synonymous; that the fresh new word, by the 200th repetition, has lost its freshness; that the enjoyable differences between boys and girls were known, yea, even by their parents, which is one reason the teen-agers are around. But few parents have been able to get the message over, and usually they can only hang tough and stick with it.

Not that some teen-agers don't have a touchingly hard time being teen-agers. One of them asked me the other day if my little girl had some stuffed animals around that she wasn't using. Teenage girls are supposed to like stuffed animals, she explained, and she didn't have any.

* Not a schoolteacher's.

I did my research for this chapter mainly in the combat area —making my own mistakes, observing little children, talking with mothers who didn't concern themselves with sibling rivalry and middle-child syndromes, but just raised good kids. And I found that the etiquette points often overlooked by the Party of the First Part and the Party of the Second Part coincidentally number the same: a generous baker's dozen.

13 THINGS PARENTS SHOULD DO, OR STOP DOING

1. *Let a child know* IN DETAIL *what you expect him to do.* Because children are sticklers for rules. Just watch them play: One toe over the chalk line and you're dead. They want to know what the rules are, and just what's going to happen— especially when you take them somewhere. A clear one-two-three explanation can help short-circuit the "Are we going to stay for dinner?" and the "I'm hungry, why can't we eat *now?*"* I checked a four-year-old boy on this point. He explained that it's hellishly difficult to rise to a social occasion when one has had no previous warning as to what the occasion is going to involve, particularly in view of one's own somewhat extensive lack of previous social experience. I thought he put it very well.

2. *Don't tag along into his world unless you're sure he wants you to.* Some kids do, some don't. Sometimes it takes a sensitive eye and heart to know whether they're glad you're aboard or wish you'd get lost. Until my daughter was seven, she was ashamed of me, and didn't want me on the nursery-school or kindergarten premises. But then I lost my luck. I am being cooperative, though, for I think it's probably best to let kids call the shots here. Their self-confidence ebbs and flows like the tides, and they know better than you do when they need you.

3. *Quit insulting him, as though he were deaf, in front of other people.* "Your hands are filthy." "Look at that face!" Many a well-meaning mother hands out a dozen insults a day, then wonders why her child grows up showing a certain ruth-

* Also, it's good to take along cookies and something to drink for your little child when you take him visiting. Your hostess may not have child-type refreshments available. Even if she does, she may be a little tired of having her pantry stripped bare in this fashion.

less lack of tact, himself. Nor are fat compliments much better. Then the little one may start to believe he's the constant center of attention, or ought to be, and this, presently, can make *you* uncomfortable. Then, too, it's poor business to talk about horrendous subjects before a tiny child, assuming he won't understand. He'll understand your tone of voice, all right, and his safe, solid world may be shaken, which will happen soon enough, when he learns to read the papers. I see no good reason to hurry it along. And guests could do a little better in their conversational efforts. They say, "What a great big girl you're getting to be!" If she's a chubby or tall-for-her-age little girl, she can feel crushed. Or furious. It is a credit to all little girls that more of them don't reply, "I'll bet you're pushing a size forty-four yourself."*

4. *Let him know that pain is sometimes unavoidable.* This lesson can keep him, one day, from biting a dentist, and if this isn't a fundamental point of etiquette, I don't know what is. (See also page 139.)

5. *Really listen when he tries to tell you something he thinks is important.* That's just good manners with anyone.

6. *Co-operate with his burgeoning good manners.* There are many heart-warming moments in raising a child, like the moment he learns to cut his own meat, so that you can cut your own before it congeals to the plate. Another is when he makes a lovely, unprompted, courteous gesture. Hence, when a five-year-old male puts out a manly hand to shake yours, get your own hand out there *fast*. If you don't, his will hang there larger than life-size, and he'll never again trust his dad, who told him to do it in the first place.

7. *Don't belabor him for not saying "Thank you" when a guest brings him a gift.* It's to be hoped that he will. But if his mind is elsewhere—and a child's mind is sometimes in a lovely Elsewhere that we've forgotten all about—or if he is bedazzled by the gift, he may not remember his Magic Words. If he doesn't, let it go. Urging the child embarrasses the guest. As a tactful guest once said, under these circumstances, "But he thanked me with his smile!"

8. *When you take him on a jolly toot, let him think it's as much for your pleasure as his.* The grim "I'm doing this for

* I am glad to note that cheek-pinching seems to be on its way out. Men used to do this to little girls. It disarranged the hair, and it even hurt. I can state unreservedly that little girls hate to have their cheeks pinched.

your sake so *enjoy* it!" approach is bad manners as well as a miserable pain in the neck to anyone, any age, any time. So let him think you, too, are having a high old time feeding the penguins (which is fun, at that). Then when you arrive home again you can feel perfectly justified in organizing a good game like Let's See Who Can Go Longest Without Speaking or Moving.

9. *Don't laugh at him unless he understands why.* It's terribly upsetting to anyone to be laughed at when he doesn't understand the joke.

10. *Adopt some minor form of public discipline.* When a public reprimand is necessary, the French *"tais-toi"* or the Spanish *"callate"* sound better than the American "shut up," but they still deliver the message. It's wise, too, to perfect a Family Look—perhaps the narrowed eye and the compressed nostril. This can mean any of a hundred things from "Be sure to thank Mrs. W. for a lovely lunch" to "Stick your shirttail in."

11. *Don't give more than two of your children names that start with the same letter. If you already have, nickname them.* Some families with numerous children major in one initial, like J: Jamie, June, Johnny, Jeanie, Joanie. Or P: Patty, Polly, Penny, Peter, Paul. This is mighty cute, but it is disconcerting to outsiders, who are never sure just which one is which, but are embarrassed to admit it. And being confused with his brothers and sisters all the time may make the child feel like a numeral and grow up antisocial, which makes for very poor etiquette sometimes.

12. *Don't teach a little child to call your grown-up friends Aunt This or Uncle That.* It can lead to an embarrassing hiatus when the child grows older and learns he's not really related to them. For these child-adult relationships, the Italian language has a lovely solution: *comare* (ko-*mahr*-ay) for a woman, *compare* (comb-*pahr*-ay) for a man. The closest approximation to the meaning of both is "dearest friend." Your child would address your friend as *"Comare,"* and in speaking *of* her, would say *"Comare* Lucy." And if these words lie uneasy on the tongue, there is still nothing the matter with Mrs. This and Mr. That.

13. *Don't assume your daughter* tells you everything, any more than you tell her everything.*

_____

* Or a son, either, although with boys the assumption isn't so often made.

". . . Kitty did in fact conceal her new views and feelings from her mother. She concealed them not because she did not respect or did not love her mother, but simply because she was her mother. She would have revealed them to anyone sooner than to her mother." —LEO TOLSTOY

If you can arrive at a point where she thinks she conceivably could tell you all, without having the roof fall in, you're doing very well indeed. An experienced mother of three beautiful daughters told me what she considers the best way to achieve this enviable state of affairs: No matter what she tells you, at whatever age, never admit to being shocked.

Then there's one other thing. It's bad form, as well as a great bore, for an adult to kick too vigorously against the traces of the changing world and reproach the child for being shaped by it. ("When *I* was a kid, *I* didn't have a bike when I was only eight years old, no *sir*.") For, really, the child can't help it. He's learning different things, about a different world, differently. Which may be all to the good.

(This occurred to me once, as I worried over the big differences between my child's upbringing and mine. But—I reflected further—I turned out thus and so, and I'm bound to admit I've met those who feel that there remains just the tiniest bit of room for improvement in the product. Ever since that time, I've held this in mind.)

And now let's consider the other side of the fence.

"I love children, especially when they cry, for then someone takes them away." —NANCY MITFORD

You may have run across the well-publicized notion that children's manners can be fun. This is unrealistic. There is nothing fun about wiping the nose, but it is a basic of children's etiquette. Every child should learn to do so as soon as he can get his hand up to it—which, as most parents will attest, happens at a remarkably early age.

Moreover, if you make everything a game, it may well remain a game in the child's mind, without getting translated into reality. The world is full of literal-minded little citizens. When Daddy and Mommy play Mr. and Mrs. Stranger who need introducing, he'll do fine. But comes along a real flesh-and-blood Mrs. Hofstedter who needs introducing, little Epaminondas will probably hang his head and dig his toes in the dirt.

Today everything is sweetened up: aspirin (orange flavor); arithmetic (baby ducklings on a pond); policemen (ice cream cones and jolly stories); doctors (balloons and magic rings)—and all this candy coating can be hard on the spiritual teeth. Some things you do because you have to, that's all, and making a game of it wastes time.

13 THINGS CHILDREN SHOULD LEARN, AND THE SOONER THE BETTER

1. *To say "Please" and "Thank you."* You can entwine these words with the word "Mama" or Mommy" at the same time he learns them. You have him say "Please, Mommy" when he wants something, or he doesn't get it, and "Thank you, Mommy" when he does. This way he'll have them down pat at the age of two or two and a half, which will amaze your friends, and pave the way for "You're welcome"—a subtler concept which comes later and doesn't matter so much anyway.

2. *To go to the toilet immediately before going anywhere else.* That is, out to play, over to the neighbor's, to school, or anywhere at all. This will save legwork for everyone.

3. *To stop* INTERRUPTING. Unless it's a naturally reticent child—and there do not seem to be as many of them around as there used to—this takes doing. For one thing, you can give him a good example to follow, by remembering to apologize when you interrupt *him*. For another, you can try to see that he gets a fair chance to be heard. At the table you can give each a turn to talk about What Was the Most Interesting (Worst, Best) Thing That Happened to Me Today, or some other sprightly subject. An egg timer can measure his minutes. But this won't accomplish much. You'll still have to nag, scream, and stomp, but you must do it. Constant interrupting is perfectly awful. (And don't be afraid he'll stop loving you because of your tantrums. The heart has its own curious reasons. Once I asked a little girl what she loved best about her mother, and after considerable thought, she said, "She makes such loud noises when I scare her.")

4. *How to tell a fair Social Lie.* Nearly any child can learn quickly to distinguish a Good Lie (told to save people's feelings) from a Bad Lie (told to keep himself out of hot water), once the difference is pointed out. A firm grasp of it will prevent his saying, "Heck, I've already got two of 'em" when he

opens a gift, or "No, it's icky" when his hostess inquires if he likes his lunch.

5. *To make no unpleasant personal remarks about people.* I found this easy to teach, and I recommend my method. You point out, from a safe distance, an odd-looking person—say, a great big fat man. Then, to your four-year-old, you say, "Look at that great big fat man. But we'd NEVER say that in FRONT of him, would we, because he'd feel ba-a-ad and he'd cry-y-y"—or whatever your own brand of pig Latin is. This really registered with my own child. Indeed, I doubt if she'd tell the neighbors their house was afire, for fear it would hurt their feelings.

Of course, this goes for unpleasant personal questions, too. His mother's yellow-haired friend may turn up red- or blue-haired tomorrow, and he must learn to roll with these punches, quietly. Then there are the outward manifestations of old age. "He is OLD, Junior. That's why his face is so wrinkled. And his bones are thin and brittle, and that's why he leans on a cane. So don't ASK." Junior may as well learn early that he'll probably end up in similar shape. After all, we're going to be either quite old or dead, one of these days, which isn't much of a choice, but there it is.

Also, you can make it plain that he doesn't talk about private things in public: family things, financial things, anatomical things. This can help prevent bad moments like the one at the church wedding, when the groom kissed the bride, and the little child asked, with clarity, "Mommy, is he planting the seed now?"

Indeed, children can learn at an early age one of the golden rules of good manners: When in doubt, keep the mouth closed.

6. *To state a preference when he is offered a choice.* When his birthday-party hostess says, "Would you like orange juice or milk?" he must say which. His hostess has both, or she wouldn't have asked. She couldn't care less which he picks, just so he picks. (Similarly, he'd better learn NOT to sound off, away from home, about his dislikes in food. When five-year-old Peewee announces, with dessert, "I hate chocolate ice cream," his hostess doesn't think, "How cute." If Peewee is going to be that hard to please, he's just not going to get around much.)

7. *To make a simple introduction.* At the age of four, he can get the fundamentals. When he learns to say, "Mommy, this is Jimmy," he has the whole thing in essence: simplicity, with the honored name said first. He can pick up the refinements later.

8. *To call most adults Mr. and Mrs. Somebody, not Steve and Mary.* If you encourage a child to call your friends by their first names, you needn't wonder why he never stands up when grownups enter the room. It is nice, too, if you can drill into his little head the merits of saying, "Yes, Mrs. So-and-so," once in a while, instead of a flat "Yes," or "Uh-huh."

9. *To write his own thank-you letters at Christmas and birthdays.* As soon as he learns to print, he can do a simple THANK YOU, AUNT DOTTIE on a piece of paper. Then you can address it and mail it. Bend that twig.

10. *To ask to help when he's a house guest.* Set or unset the table. Carry things. Fetch things. Make a pass at making his own bed.

11. *To stay out of other people's private business.* Rooms, drawers, closets. And mail. As soon as he can read, he'd better learn not to read other people's letters or what curls out of people's typewriters. (Of course, he won't ever learn this if his parents do it, or if he ever catches Mommy perusing the diary he'd carefully hidden behind his old baseball suit in his bottom dresser drawer. This is excruciatingly bad parental etiquette, and Mommy deserves a good ducking in the town pond.) This is only basic good manners. Also, people who do it are apt to read something unflattering about themselves, as many an older child from 20 to 90 has learned to his discomfiture.

12. *Never to answer the telephone with "Who's this?"* He can learn, early, to say "Smiths' house."

13. *To understand that some people will like him better than others do.* The wound won't go so deep, the first time he's left out of a party, if he realizes that some people may not even like him at all, just as *he* doesn't like some people at all. He must know that some friendships sour, some shift, some dissolve, some grow, some endure—among which is yours, because you love him. Unreservedly and invincibly, and come what may.

"... *For children once settled and confident can mostly be left, it seems, to manage their difficulties without us. Only what we must do, always and unalterably, is hold their hand firmly in general goodwill. Then they themselves seem to deal with their own particular troubles far better than we can. In any case we do not know how to help them in any more definite way.*" —NAN FAIRBROTHER

CHAPTER TWELVE

All Those Other People:
An Alphabetiquette

"We walked up to Times Square along 44th Street. Where the big trucks bring the rolls of paper into the Times I said Hello to the guy in the uniform that stands around there all the time and he said 'How they going?' and I said 'Okay.'
" 'Who's that guy?' Sam said.
" 'He's the man I say Hello to,' I said."

—RICHARD BISSELL

ARTISTS

Performers love applause, which is one reason they perform. So it is impolite to sit on your hands through a performance, even though the concert soprano, say, leaves something to be desired. Anyway, huzzahs are vitamins, and given enough of them she may hit the high C yet.

People are often reluctant to intrude backstage with congratulations, or at the speaker's platform. But it is seldom an intrusion. Nearly always, performers are pleased and grateful.

Should you become involved with a concert arrangement—for instance, a Community Concert with a visiting female artist—it's sound practical etiquette to be sure a strip of carpet (or even butcher paper) leads from the wings to stage center. Otherwise, her long dress gets dirty, and dry cleaning on tour is an expensive nuisance.

Pianists like an adjustable bench or stool, too. It is a sorry thing to have to slip around on a stack of phone books, which some fine short pianists have had to do.

Most evening performers, especially singers, like to eat afterward. Usually they've last eaten around 5:00 P.M., and by 11:00 P.M. they are dying of hunger. So gadgety canapés and *petits-fours* aren't as good for the postconcert reception as hearty food and, often, whisky.

In asking artist-friends to perform—design a Christmas card, sing at a wedding, or whatever—it's good manners to make it immediately clear whether this is for love or for money, and if it is for money, how much. And it's best not to ask for free performances of any nature, unless you're sure of your ground. Work's work.

And artists shouldn't be bashful about stating fees. It is easy to do as a well-known Victorian critic did. "I've a 30-guinea speech and a three-guinea speech," he'd say, and pause. "But I really can't recommend the three-guinea speech."

BARTENDERS

"How to Humor a Bar-Tender

"1. Mumble what you want to drink and be sure to argue when the drink comes. Argue anyway, you might get a free one.

"2. Put lighted cigarette on bar so that it will burn the wood, as ash trays are a mere decoration.

"3. Never lay money down on bar until asked for price, then claim you've paid.

4. Bang on the bar when you want service. It looks smart and makes you feel tough.

"*5. Always be sure to scream after every second drink, 'Don't the house ever pop?'*"

—FROM THE COCKTAIL NAPKIN
AT CHUCK AND EDIE'S

CATERERS

The woman behind the coffee urn at the big reception is probably a caterer, with much on her mind. While she busily fills 300 cups with coffee, she'd rather no one asked for Sanka. "Anybody needs caffeineless coffee, fine, or saccharine, fine, so long as he brings it himself," as one caterer explained it, with clarity.

Caterers run into funny questions, most of which get right down to basic etiquette. Mrs. Social de Zastre, a guest at Mrs. Hoy T. Toity's catered affair, will actually ask the caterer just how much he's charging per guest. Of course, the caterer won't rat. Or she'll ask him the recipe of that interesting artichoke-bottom-and-mushroom dish. And of course she won't get it: the caterer's recipes are his capital.

Now, it's to be hoped that

1. Mrs. Toity, the hostess, had the good sense and manners to leave the caterer *alone,* instead of suggesting that she whittle the carrot strips this way, and

2. that she had plenty of soap flakes and clean towels available, plus an empty dishwasher (the caterer will probably use it for storing, not for washing, but it should still be empty) and denuded kitchen counters, when the caterers came marching in. The make-ready isn't part of their job. Neither is general housework. A caterer I know was greeted by the hostess with "Check and see if the beds are made, and be sure there are clean towels in the bathroom." This so bemused the caterer that she actually did it, but she's still going around talking to herself.

DENTISTS

Most dentists are more long-suffering than their patients, this day of the swift novocaine needle.

It is true that all dentists should have marvelous breaths, but so should all patients. The patient who makes his after-lunch dental date, without first using a potent mouthwash, shows a faulty grasp of etiquette's practical rudiments.

Another problem of dentists is hangovers, mainly those which belong to the patient. With a hangover, anything hurts, including a kind look. The patient should have postponed the dental appointment or the hangover, one or the other.

A dentist is as happy as dentists were ever destined to be when a mother reads the old magazines in the waiting room while her child is in the dental chair. If she's beside him, little Jimmy will raise more Cain. He and the dentist, left alone, will reach a certain rapport, if only because Jimmy realizes he is a sitting duck.

And the dentist is even happier, if that be possible, when Mother doesn't tell Jimmy beforehand that the dentist is a nice man who won't hurt him one little bit. For this may make a liar of Mother and a brute of the dentist, who may *have* to hurt him one little bit. The dentist would like to treat Jimmy as a person instead of an infant, but Mother can make it hard.

Mixing business with pleasure is another black mark on the part of the layman. "My third molar's coming in—what should I do about it?" isn't so good at the cocktail table.

However, in the area of people versus dentists, the worst blooper is made by the patient who announces immediately that he simply hates dentists. (While admiring his bravery, one must deplore his manners.) A far better approach is that of a lady I know, who plumps herself happily into a new dentist's chair, beaming trustfully. "I've never had a dentist hurt me in my life!" she says. "And I know you won't be the first!"

EVERYONE BEHIND A COUNTER

The big thing is to *look* at salespeople. As though they are, not inanimate objects or numbers, but people. Not only is this fundamental courtesy, it saves time and trouble when you remember it was the little blue-eyed woman in the jersey who's gone looking for your size 12 in the green.

Indeed, practical manners abound in the store-etiquette picture. The customer at the check-out stand who remarks to the clerk packing her groceries, "My, it takes *know-how* to pack things properly, doesn't it!" is less apt to find the eggs scrambled with the apricots when she gets the brown bagful home.

Consider the proper tactics when you've been short-changed, or think you have. It's polite—and wise—to say, "Wait a minute—I'm afraid you've gypped yourself!" Then you figure it out together, and—surprise—he has gypped *you*. But he isn't embarrassed now as he makes amends.

When you give your address, it saves time and erasures for the salesclerk if you say Two-Oh-One-Five instead of Twenty-Fifteen. Transcribing Twenty-Fifteen demands a doublethink.

Salespeople, too, have their imperatives. They shouldn't call women Honey or correct their pronunciation:

"Where is the lingerie department, please?"

"You mean lahn-jer-ay?"

Luxury shops can pose problems. When Mrs. Shortacash finds herself in a shop where the prices are only slightly higher than the saleswoman's nose, she feels she must work her way out of this one. Often she'll mumble something about "No, I can't wear that neckline (or that color, or that sort of a peplum)."

But this fools no one. That saleslady wasn't born yesterday, dearie. The word is already out in the back room that Mrs. S. won't pay price (classic rag-trade lingo for the woman whose eyes bulge more than her billfold).

What Mrs. Shortacash *should* have said was, "Really, that's more than I'd thought of paying. Fifty dollars is my absolute limit." It is remarkable how this can humanize salesladies, who'll sometimes put their hearts into finding something among the markdowns. At the very least, there's no mutual embarrassment, with both of you knowing you're lying.

One ruse is handy to know, though, when you want to look around in an antique shop, for instance, and find that it is richer than you are. Usually, antique people are happy to have you look. But should you detect crispness in the "May I help you?" you should have at the ready some reasonably unfindable object you are seeking. My own favorite is old Swedish *bobêches*. (If the shop happens to have some, they're just not old enough.)

FIRST-NAMERS

The first-namer (or nicknamer) picks his way along a path perilous with landmines.

Done to well-known people, first-naming suggests false intimacy—quite as dismal as false elegance. And if the first-namer gets the name wrong, as he so often does, it is a dead giveaway. (Maybe Margaret Actress is known to her intimates not as Marge, but as Peg, Margo, or Pigsy.) Where plain or unfamous people are concerned, the first-namer runs the risk of offending his new acquaintance (who probably won't *tell* him, however, that he considers it an invasion of privacy, because he is too polite).

Therefore, when someone says, "John Johnson, this is William Firstnamer," Firstnamer had better say, "How do you do, Mr. Johnson"—especially if Johnson is noticeably older. If Mr. Johnson hungers for more intimacy, he can so inform Mr. Firstnamer.

". . . I do not take it as a degradation of my dignity to be called George by a stranger, even by a young man of thirty-five. I just want it to mean something.

". . . I propose that anyone who calls me George the first time we meet should be prepared to recognize me the next time. I do not want to be introduced all over again, even if our next meeting takes place years later. This possibility should be foreseen: if the circumstances of our first meeting are so casual as to indicate that we may well never meet again, let us by all means call each other Mr., literally once and for all." GEORGE STEVENS

GENTLEMEN

Gentlemen are men who are gentle in their relationships with other people, especially people weaker, poorer, or in some other fashion less favored than they. A gentleman, it has been truly said, hurts no one's feelings unintentionally.

HANDICAPPED PERSONS

It's important to good etiquette to realize that everyone is handicapped in some way or other, but in some people it shows more.

According to physically handicapped people, what they *don't* want is a big dollop of sympathy. This makes them feel sorrier for themselves than they do already (and almost any honest handicapped person will admit he has his low moments). Nor do they want undue solicitude. If a cripple is about to open the door for himself, let him do it; don't leap to his aid. If he opens the door for you, a casual "Thank you" is sufficient.

Speak to a blind person before you touch him. Let him take

your arm, generally speaking, instead of your taking his. He knows when he needs it.

Also, well-mannered or even ordinarily bright people won't assume that because someone is handicapped in one department, he's handicapped in others. Deaf people can *see,* blind people can *hear,* crippled people can see and hear and feel. Indeed, all handicapped people can feel, and do. They feel like people, and want to be treated so.

Take the case of a well-known professional man—who happened to be blind—at a banquet with his wife. The waiter said to his wife, "Would your husband care for more chicken?" Understandably annoyed, the blind man snapped back, "Now, how the hell would *she* know if I want more chicken?"

A blind friend of mine went to the welfare office, with her son, to fill out the various required forms. The clerk found the blanks, snapped open his pen, then said to the son, "Now, where was your mother born?" "If you'd ask her," the son replied coldly, "she might tell you."

INTERIOR DECORATORS

Interior decorators have problems, among which are scrapbooks, invasion of privacy, and sneakiness, these three. But the greatest of these is scrapbooks.

For years, the client has clipped pretty pictures, you see, and she wants her bedroom to be a montage of them all (though the decorator must work around the golden-oak bed and dresser). But it's impolite to put such hurdles in a professional's pathway, and also impractical. The end result may well look like the production of a not-very-bright committee, and gladden no hearts.

A better approach would be "Could you do something about this funny bedroom? Unfortunately we must keep the bed and dresser." A good decorator will then take it from there, proceeding on the basis of her client's tastes as they're reflected in her personality and the rest of the house.

A woman often feels cozy toward her decorator, as toward her obstetrician, and for similar reasons. They are involved, she feels, in a big mutual production. So she'll telephone him at home—weekends, evenings, or at 7:00 A.M.—to ponder aloud over the toile versus the stripe. This is pretty bad-mannered, except in times of crisis, with the painters waiting and not a color swatch in sight.

And this cozy feeling can unwittingly lead to sneakiness. (Indeed, ethics and etiquette become ethiquette here, as thoroughly mixed as the yolk and the white of a scrambled egg.) What can happen is this: The lady invites her good friend-and-decorator to cocktails or dinner. Then—because her uninspired guest room is uppermost in her mind—she brings it up. But Martinis and dinner don't equal the decorator's proper consultation fee of $10 an hour or higher (while $25 is usually the initial charge for looking things over the first time). Incidentally, because decorators make their money through buying at wholesale and selling at retail, they make none when clients confer with them, then do their own purchasing. When the client does so, as sometimes happens, he'd better remember he's bought consultation time, anyway.

JESTERS

The jester needn't preface his joke with an "Oops—wait a minute—is anyone here Irish (or vegetarian, or whatever it is)?" This isn't particularly good manners, it's merely admitting that the jester may have some privately naughty attitudes toward Irishmen or vegetarians but doesn't want to give himself away in the enemy camp. Better just tell it if it's a good joke, and not tell it if it isn't. He should, however, have ready a bridge or transitional topic to throw in the minute the joke's over, so the conversation won't just lie there. While—often—someone will tell another joke in a trice, it can sometimes be the longest trice you ever sat through.

KINFOLK

Kinfolk should pay twice the attention friends do to Visiting Rules (Chapter 2), and the fact that many don't is what gives them a bad name. When houses were big, elastic, many-storied, many-peopled affairs, relatives could suddenly land on relatives with comparatively little pain. But now, with so many houses built to measure, and the guest room often the family room as well, one can't count on free lodgings in Winnetka just because a married brother lives there.

Mothers-in-law, among kinfolk, pose a special problem: what to call them. And really, it's their job to solve it, remembering that most people know only one person whom they can naturally call "Mother."

The old-fashioned "Mother Jones" seems too long, to some

people, or too rural, or too stuffy. And "Claire"—if that is her first name—may seem too flip.

If she likes, a mother-in-law can choose a new name to be used for this new relationship. She might revive her middle name and be Anne to her new son- or daughter-in-law. Or Mac, if her maiden name is McKinley.

But she'd better do *something,* or her new child-in-law will be stumbling around with no convenient handle. The future grandchildren will, of course, solve the problem eventually, but it may be with "Bapoo" or "Binky" (all right for grandchildren but a little cute for grownups).

LADIES

The traits of a gentleman apply here, for gallantry knows no sex. However, the word "lady" is somewhat out of favor. Many a woman would rather be thought womanly than a lady, which has acquired overtones of smelling salts and screaming at snakes. Yet, a true lady is as lovely a phenomenon as she is hard to define, though a start is made by the old rule: A lady is a woman in whose presence a man is a gentleman.

In a downtown department store, once, two young women entered the elevator on the tenth floor. An elderly man entered, too, and promptly removed his hat. The elevator stopped on Nine. Then on Eight. Then on Seven. At this point, one of the young women turned to the other and growled, "Hell, this damn thing's stopping on every floor." Quietly, then, without a change of expression, the elderly man put his hat back on.

M.D.'S AND ANALYSTS

"You haven't called me Doc and you haven't asked for any free medical advice, so you can join me at bourbon time any day."

—JOHN D. MACDONALD

And of course you don't write "Dr. Jekyll" in addressing an envelope to him or writing a check, for this would magically turn him into a dentist.* The envelope is addressed, simply,

> Lancelot Jekyll, M.D.
> Holesville
> Utah

---

* This is the way you *do* address a dentist: Dr. I. Pulham.

The formal salutation on the letter inside the envelope repeats this, then begins, "Dear Dr. Jekyll:" Your check, too, is made out to Lancelot Jekyll, M.D.—although, should he misdiagnose your pleurisy as athlete's foot, and in a fit of pique you make your check out to Lancelot Jekyll, Doctor of Veterinary Medicine, he will cash it.

But if this sort of misdiagnosis continues, it is obvious that a certain rapport is lacking between you, and you'd better go elsewhere. He may well be as tired of the whole thing as you are—after all, he is in the business of curing people—so this poses no major etiquette problem. You simply say, one day while he is looking at you and scratching his head, "You know, Dr. Jekyll, I've always had a hunch it's my adenoids that make me look like this, and for my own peace of mind I think I'd better go elsewhere (or get another opinion)." Then you ask him to send the pertinent data in your file to the new doctor whose pleasure you are about to become. (It's best not to do this *until* you know what doctor you're going to, because in case of an emergency you'd be up the crick.)

It might be said here—in fact, it *will* be said here—that this is the procedure to follow in changing lawyers, dentists, or any sort of regular services, professional or otherwise. When you leave your hairdresser of some months' standing for another whose location is more convenient, or replace a yardman who has been overcharging and underworking, it is only fair to say why, in a pleasant but firm fashion. Anyone whose services are summarily dispensed with becomes confused—what did he do wrong?—and resentful. And if he *did* do something wrong, learning what it was may help him to do better in the future.

> *"Three things that constitute a physician: a complete cure; leaving no blemish behind; a painless examination."*
> — The Triads of Ireland 9TH CENTURY

Analysts have their problems, too, which is only fair, now I think about it. Still, it's poor manners to add to anyone's if you can help it. It would be nice if more people would leave their ids and their kids' ids at home when they go to a social affair where an analyst is apt to be. Most analysts* don't want to

* Some analysts use their curious professional calling as an excuse to be prodding and provocative on social occasions. This is no good, either.

work around the clock, but often they're not allowed to forget their calling for a minute.

Just as numerous are the people who self-consciously clam up on finding they're talking to an analyst, for fear of revealing something colorful.

If there were a happy medium, analysts would be a happier crew.

NURSES

It is poor form to kick the nurse for what the doctor did or ordered. Nurses are mostly marvelous: some of them beautiful, many of them wise, all of them doing things that have to be done, and if you don't think so, change doctors (see page 145).

Nurses like candy. Persuade your friends to switch some of their business from the florist to the candy store. Then leave the chocolate box open. Your light gets answered faster that way.

OLD PEOPLE

For years there has been a dreadful movement afoot to prevent people from growing old with dignity: to keep them, instead, in a dreary no man's land of spurious youth, blue hair, and bingo, with a young man from Arthur Murray's coming over to The Home every Saturday night to lead the frolic. (It has come to my shuddering attention—and I regretfully pass the information along—that somewhere in this broad land of ours is a retirement home named Youngland). It is true that some older people and old people enjoy all this. It is equally true that some do not. Good manners in getting along with them consists of discerning who does and who doesn't, and acting accordingly.

A woman I know was worried about her mother. "Mother, you seem so dim and far away," she said. "What is the problem?" The old lady smiled. "There isn't any problem, dear," she said. "You just won't let me sit and be eighty-eight."

PART-TIME HELP

A better name is Household Employees. And the woman who comes in, periodically, to clean, isn't the char or the scrublady.

She is the cleaning woman or the housekeeper-by-the-day. A sense of dignity encourages anyone to do a better job.

The big etiquette books give much valuable information on the subject: how to organize the work, what to expect, and so on. But you just ought to read how you're supposed to address her, and introduce her. When Mrs. Lardly P. Esplanade introduces Mrs. Robert Hennessy—her maid, cook, housekeeper-by-the-day, or whathaveyou—to Miss Visitor, she doesn't give Mrs. Hennessy the dignity of her married name. No *sir*. She says, "Miss Visitor, this is our Emmy—she'll be glad to help you," after which I suppose Mrs. Esplanade throws Emmy a dog biscuit and whistles her back under the couch.

Presently, then, Mrs. Esplanade will go write a club paper on the difficulty of getting domestic help these days, and how ungrateful they all are. Emmy had enjoyed absolutely every advantage, too, in the three weeks she stayed.

QUAINT PEOPLE, QUEER PEOPLE

"Whenever the world gets so there's nobody out of the ordinary in it no more, it'll be a pretty sad old world, that's all I can say! A pretty sad old world." —ARDYTH KENNELLY

RICH PEOPLE

Rich people shouldn't turn themselves inside out to act like poor people, because this makes poor people angry. No good etiquette can result.

For instance, when rich people invite poor people to dinner, they needn't think the poor people would be happier eating their plain old chipped beef, because they wouldn't. The poor people expect a little pizazz. Chipped beef belongs on a chipped plate, not on Limoges, and the poor people know this. So the rich people can save their chipped beef for their rich friends, who can be expected to understand the rigors of living in the thinner ozone of the Northern Brackets. But their poor friends should be served steak.

They shouldn't underdress for their poor friends, either. It doesn't make Judy O'Grady angry when she sees the Colonel's lady in superb vicuña. She thinks, admiringly, "Boy, that's what *I'd* get, too!" But if the Colonel's lady takes trouble to look terrible, whacking her denim pants off at the knee with rusty scissors, Judy thinks she's dressing down to her level, and she'd like to poke her one.

SAD PEOPLE

See Chapters 13 and 14.

TRAVEL AGENTS

Travel agents are knowing and noble. A travel agent understands psychological subtleties. He understands that if you, yourself, discover a picturesquely dreadful Mexican fleabag, you may like it, but if he'd sent you there, you'd sue him for damages.

And he knows some gloomier facets. An occasional customer will demand a lively itinerary from Chicago to New Zealand with 14 stopovers, get the rough draft, then comparison-shop at another travel bureau down the street to beat the price (not knowing that T.A.'s are a friendly crew, and word gets around).

Yet he works unceasingly at producing bang-up trips for everybody, which would be simpler to do if some of his customers would, for one thing, admit their ignorance. Which can be hard, if Mrs. Phileas Fogg has *been* to Paris once, and dreams of staying again at that mad, gay little Left Bank hotel. But the T.A. knows (from his incredibly efficient spy system) that the little hotel isn't mad and gay any more, it's just mad, as Mrs. Fogg will be if he puts her up there. He will do so if she insists. But it is unkind to force him into doing something so greatly against his better professional judgment.

Mrs. Fogg should be honest, too, about her money, habits, and health. She needn't be embarrassed to admit that $1,200 is the size of her travel budget. She'd better *say* whether she really wants to do more pub-crawling than sight-seeing, or vice versa. If she gets carsick, or can't climb stairs or stand elevators, she'd better tell him loud and clear.

Finally, Mrs. Fogg should understand that the Travel Agent receives his compensation from prearrangements with many hotels and most transportation companies (the latter being the larger part). But if she's had him revise her itinerary four times, and then canceled the trip, he may charge a cancellation fee for his time. Some do, some don't. If he doesn't, it would be mannerly if she'd ask to pay the cost of the wires and airmail letters. (Because making and canceling an airmail reservation in the Orient, for example, costs the agent about $1.25, all in all, and Mrs. Fogg is the one who messed up the plans, and fair's fair, and etiquette's etiquette, and pigs is pigs.)

ULTRABENEVOLENT PEOPLE

They put 50¢ into the cripple's cup but don't take the pencil they just bought, thus turning a wistful business into a charity operation and proving their manners need an overhaul, all in one fell swoop.

VETERINARIANS

People are usually polite to veterinarians because veterinarians are polite to their dogs, cats, and birds. Their main etiquette error is beefing over the cost of the medicine. Not the cost of the surgery (because they usually seem to understand that it took skill to cut Ming Toy open and sew her up again so she would go on ticking), just the cost of the antibiotics. Veterinarians would like their clientele to understand that puppy pills cost as much as people pills, so hush up.

WRITERS

Writers become unhappier than usual when asked if they are still writing. All writers write, whether or not they are published. And when the question follows a smash sale, it merely confirms the writer's dark suspicion that his book had, after all, the resounding impact of a feather on a snowbank. Another depressant is "I *loved* your book—I've loaned it to everyone I know!" So is "Where do you get your ideas?" because there is no sensible short answer.

It's mistaken manners to ask a writer to judge a manuscript. It won't flatter him, it will bother him; he has trouble enough judging his own. Publishers publish, editors criticize and edit, agents criticize and sell, writers write. That's the way it goes.

A curious thing is this: Friends and acquaintances will sometimes ask writers, "What'd they pay you for that?"—though they'd never ask the question of other people. It leads the writer —understandably enough—to triple the figure, thus contributing to the Rich Oddball Writer mystique. When the questioner sees him six months later, still with holes in his socks and driving his 1953 Plymouth, he thinks fondly, "What a character."

CHAPTER THIRTEEN

Gifts and Gentle Deeds

*"This is a present because it's Spring
and you're so pretty."*
—KATHLEEN'S UNCLE DALE

This note accompanied the ribbon-knit dress, and you could
look far and do worse when it comes to the Present Perfect,
perfectly presented. Uncle Dale knew what he was about, and
so did Aunt Lorraine, who undoubtedly chose the dress (you
know how men are) and wrapped it up. For here it is: a pretty
thought and a pretty thing, the gift and the giver, kindness
touched with romance, all in a sudden April package.

But before we get carried away, we'd better face up to what this chapter is about: It is about Gifts—the etiquette and theory of them, with some hopefully helpful suggestions—and about kindly things to do for people. These tend to run into each other, because any gentle deed is a gift, of time, or attentiveness, or thought, or money—any or all. Still, one must get organized and draw a line somewhere, or one wouldn't get anything done.

Now, in considering good presents, let's keep in mind Uncle Dale's to Kathleen, while remembering that no one can do so spectacularly well every time. Like the ostrich egg the farmer put in the hen house, it is only something to aim at.

First, about the romantic or sentimental quotient—especially important in gifts for women, as I learned not long ago, in making a random survey of Most Memorable Gifts. Indeed, I was only half done with it when a difference between the sexes became resoundingly clear.

A woman, for instance, can tell you right away, in neon, what gift she remembers. A man can't; he must usually scratch his chin and think. And a woman's memorable present involves, nearly always, a man. But a man's is singularly uncluttered by romance. Dollars to doughnuts, he'll dredge it up out of the misty, many-layered, womanless past, out of the brave bright days when he was a boy. The pup he got when he was seven. The fire-chief bike he got when he was ten. The dart board with real darts that went THUNK. And this is sentiment, of course, but not precisely romance. But women—

Well, take the case of a friend of mine, whose most memorable gift is a charm-bracelet charm which her husband, Joe, gave her for her birthday: an impossibly angelic silver angel, engraved on the back, "MOST OF THE TIME, LOVE, JOE." Now, this may not sound like much to a man, but it warms Amy's heart like a blowtorch. Consider, too, its valuable side effects. As a woman will perceive instantly, it gives Amy a gratifying lead in the area of female friendsmanship. A friend notices the angel at lunch, say, and asks to see it. Amy gladly hands it over. When the friend reads that message of clearly understated devotion, it sends her home in a state bordering on shock. *Her* husband never thought of anything cute like that.

This isn't to say that a woman always prefers that one perfect rose (or trinket) to that one perfect limousine. Or that a woman can't feel sentimental about mink—a generic term here for any lavish object—if she gets it at the right time from the right person.* But unfortunately it seldom works out like this. If her husband can easily afford it, it's just another coat from Daddy. (And even if he can't, there's no escaping the fact that there's something in it for him—see Sidesaddles, page 154. The cave man dragging a fur-covered object home for his wife to wear was showing the world what a mighty hunter he was, whether he was or not.)

Look, too, at the most memorable present of my cousin Alicia. Alicia loves antiques, or—more accurately—what she calls cute old things. She finds them in funny old shops or in obscure corners of the Salvation Army's collection depot. She has a special fondness for old bottles, old bootjacks, and old pickling crocks, and her husband has been heard to complain that their living room is starting to look like somebody's basement. Nevertheless, one Christmas he gave her a $25 receipt from one of the weariest of these places and told her to go buy some more. Here, if you examine it carefully, is a romantic gift indeed, for it carries with it the warming affirmation, *You're an odd duck but I love you anyway*.

The good present's second big element is uniqueness. No present should be quite like another's except in the case of little children. If Patty's new doll wears pink bootees, while Peggy's has only pink mittens, there'll be trouble, as many a mother has learned the hard way. Perhaps this is why a woman will seldom err in this fashion, while a man occasionally will. It is Christmas Eve, and as he wanders glumly through the shops, his wife and his daughter are on his mind. When he stumbles into the Christmas crop of cashmeres, he may solve his problem in a flash. Both his women like yellow, and anyway his feet hurt. So he buys two identical yellow cardigans.—Which he shouldn't have done, as he'll learn the first shopping day after Christmas, when one or the other of the yellow cashmeres is magically sea-changed into a red pull-over or an electric skillet.

(It's a shame, by the way, to exchange gifts. Still, it's wise to leave a loophole when you give them—not autograph the book till you're sure it's not a duplicate, or have the sweater monogrammed till you know it fits.)

And then there is unexpectedness: the gift you get because it's spring, or just because. This is usually more special than the gift because it's Christmas.

---

* It is nice to know that a man may properly give his fiancée a fur stole, though not a fur coat.

Also, the gift you get in addition to the one you hinted for may well be the more special of the two. I know a man who wanted a special imported fishing reel for his birthday. He thoughtfully checked it in the sportsmen's catalog and turned down the coupon page. Of course, his wife couldn't miss, and she didn't. But she gave him, as well, a handsomely framed color enlargement—a picture she'd taken when he wasn't looking—of the biggest bass he'd caught the previous season. *This* is the present he brags about.

Then there's another side to unexpectedness, a side to be wary of. On this side you find the way-out gift, or Let's Give Grandma a Brace of Falcons.

A man I know—a rather philosophical type—does this often, fondly hoping to open windows for his friends onto new vistas. He once gave his wife an ant farm—one of those glass-enclosed ant universes before which you are supposed to sit, spellbound, watching the ants go around doing whatever it is ants do. But his wife was not spellbound. She gave the ant farm to a little boy across the street who is hot for bugs.

Actually, the window-opening theory reads prettier than it works out. Most people have more open windows than they have time to look out of, as it is.

Akin to this type of gift is the one he'd never give himself (the reason being that he doesn't want it). Not that this can't be highly successful if the gift is what Billy Rose once called a Five-Dollar Cake of Soap—the absolute best-of-breed item in a category the giftee already likes. But if it is a category you think he *should like*—say, a jug of French perfume for a woman who never touches the stuff—you're in dangerous country.

Consider this woman. If she's past the age of consent, she probably cherishes a notion, deluded though it may be, that she's achieved for herself a fairly satisfactory personal style. When you give the out-and-out tweedy type a marabou trifle, you are implying, of course, "I can see the *femme fatale* peeping through that tailored exterior, and here's something to bring her out." But she may think she's a tweedy *femme fatale*, anyway, and misread the message as "Why don't you *do* something about yourself?"

These mistakes verge perilously close to the Insult Gift—the drugstore's holly-trimmed packets of toothpaste and so forth that bloom there, like poinsettias, before Christmas. The merchants' enthusiasm is commendable but misguided. Anyone who gives one of these affairs to a lady of spirit is apt to get it back across the chops.

Finally, before we go into some possible presents for problem people, let's take a brisk look at Sidesaddles and Toe-Covers.

Sidesaddles are seldom memorable. "Sidesaddle" is our family's name for that good book you give your husband because you want to read it yourself, or the croquet set which the croquet fan gives a member of the immediate family for the whole family to enjoy.

These can be good presents, mind you, but not best presents, while Toe-Covers are practically hopeless. "Toe-Cover" was Betty MacDonald's family name for those highly improbable widgets like left-handed fettucine cutters or a set of seven blue-velvet bookmarks, each dedicated to a different day of the week, which provoke from the recipient a truly sincere "You shouldn't have done it!" Toe-Covers are usually redistributed the following Christmas, if you can remember whom not to give them back to.

And so to a few suggestions about Gifts. Here we find the children—as we so often do—coming on strong.

"A truly appreciative child will break, lose, spoil, or fondle to death any really successful gift within a matter of minutes."
—RUSSELL LYNES

On occasion, that's a comforting thing to keep in mind. Still, there's another side to it. You *may* be doing a child a disservice in thinking he doesn't like something just because he doesn't break it immediately. Adults don't necessarily rush out immediately to take pictures with their new cameras or settle down instantaneously to read their new books. There is indeed a time for sowing and a time for reaping, a time for opening and a time for enjoying.

Discovering what small children want is no problem. They want whatever Uncle Buggsy on Channel 7 tells them they want, and they want it for at least half an hour after they get it. Deciding what they ought to have, however, to flavor their present stockpile of 200 talking teddy bears and 350 bright games, is another matter. In deciding this it is every man for himself.

The fact remains, a little child has more fun with the bug he caught for himself and put in an old peanut-butter jar than he does with the Pixy Nixy Bug Collectors' Kit complete with sanitized pins and educational materials. But you'd look chintzy giving your child an old peanut-butter jar for Christmas, wouldn't you now? The kid across the street got a record player.

A small child *thinks* he wants what he wants. He thinks this very hard. Therefore, with him, the unexpected seldom works. When he confidently expects to find a set of plastic bagpipes under the tree on Christmas morning and finds a xylophone instead, it will be a dreary old day until you set forth in searcₕ of a plastic-bagpipe store that is open on Christmas morning.

Also, little sick children *need* presents. They help them get well faster. A good thing to do is to pick up any interesting small items you run across, wrap them, and hide them away. Then, come flu, come measles, you can put these in a stack outside his bedroom door, strings attached to each, so that he can pull one over, every hour on the hour—or maybe every three hours. How sick is he?

And I know a mother who works good magic. When her sick child is asleep, she puts a wrapped-up object under the nightstand. When he wakes, she says a magic word, stomps around three times, and Presto Findo—there's a magic object under the nightstand. Wouldn't she be surprised if she found it under the dresser?

It's important for little children to learn about making things themselves to give away. There are many rather appalling things they can make and often do: coasters, cut with pinking shears from pieces of felt. Or lumpy pencil pots, from cheese glasses dunked in clay, then painted and studded with sequins and beads. Or pomander sachet balls—which are apples studded solidly with whole cloves—for anyone who likes his underwear to smell like apple pie. But no one cares if they're appalling, for heaven's sake, and making these things keeps him busy and thinking along the right lines.

Children can also crack walnuts carefully into neat halves, or you can. Then they insert a loop of gold wrapping cord before gluing the halves back together and gilding them. A set of a dozen matched walnuts is as nice a present as anyone could want, especially anyone who trims his Christmas tree in an artful way.

Children versus Teachers In some schools, laws are laid down, and children give their teachers no Christmas presents. Otherwise—

Well, something the child made would be best. But if he didn't make anything, it is up to Mother, as so many things are. It must be said, and this seems the logical place to say it, that teachers are tired of cheap soap and cheap cologne. They can recognize at 20 paces that stuff Aunt Franny-bless-her-heart gave you last Christmas. But a good handkerchief would be nice. Or a little box of plain note paper. Or a jar or two of Mama's homemade pickles, if she makes them, or a small boughten delicacy on the exotic side. Whatever it is, it shouldn't be too much. Like $2 maximum.

Two other sorts of people are, oddly enough, oversoaped: housekeepers-by-the-day and travelers.

Soap is certainly the last thing your cleaning woman wants to see any more of, even fancy French cakes of it. Better would be a filled-up trading-stamp book or two, if you save trading stamps. Or a pretty brocade coin purse with a green bill inside. Or ditto with a gift certificate inside, though there's no real point in pinning her down to one particular store. Or a green potted plant with some green bills tied with bright ribbon to the branches.

Travelers at *bon voyage* parties get enough wee packets of soap beads to wash the Louvre. A tiny flashlight with two extra batteries would be better. The traveler would think of you with gratitude each time he traveled down the long dark hall in that quaint old Normandy inn in search of the bathroom. Or a small pair of collapsible scissors, with a roll of cellophane tape, tucked into a coin purse. These are invaluable items for any traveler, and ones he seldom thinks to take. Or solid cologne, in any innocuous fresh scent if you don't know her taste. Or a one-pound note, dedicated to a boat ride down the Thames (or any other foreign banknote similarly earmarked). You can get it from your local bank even in a very small town, if you'll set about it early enough.

Teen-agers and Presents Here there are fewer absolutes. Still, this can be said: Don't worry about giving them the Gift They'd Never Buy for Themselves, because it's hard to think of one. Teen-agers will buy anything, given the funds, and the farther out in left field it is—generally speaking—the better; if it's the same left field their friends are in. Just see to it that whatever you pick is a year or two more sophisticated than they are.

An almost infallibly successful gift for a teen-age girl, by the way, is tarot cards or a Ouija board, or anything else of that sort which enables her to tell fortunes and be the life of the party.

Then there are the Shirt-Tail Attachments. These are people you don't know whether to give something to or not, because you don't know whether they're going to give you something or not, and nobody wants to embarrass anybody. Maybe it's an old old friendship that has worn thin. Or a rather new, spontaneous combustion-type friendship that has worn thin. Like the Chesters, from Idaho.

The Chesters, you may remember, rented the place next door at the beach, a season or so ago, and she was just lovely with the children. So, the Christmas after that summer, you sent them that sea-shell book and they sent you the barbecue forks. But last summer you didn't happen to vacation at the same place, though you corresponded. . . .

Well, in solving these abstruse situations, small homemade items can be helpful. A hand-framed snapshot of that same old beach. Or a new litter bag for their station wagon, or a beach bag.* Or the fifth hanging fuchsia basket Junior made in Manual Training during his Hanging-Fuchsia-Basket Period— something like that. These are only thoughts, you see, and thoughts don't embarrass other people the way gifts would (in case the Chesters have forgotten you completely).

People Who Have Everything   This is an ever-increasing problem, in our time, but it can usually be solved with things they can use up. Dramatic candles are good, several colors and sizes. Or a box of distinctive gift wrapping, if the lady herself is an ardent gift-giver. Or New Orleans peach leather, or Oregon wild blackberry jam, or any other regional specialty. Or tickets. If they don't like what you picked, they can still have the pleasure of giving them away.

But if you want to pick something lasting, a good place to look is in the old junk-and-second-hand stores. You might find an old calendar cake plate bearing a sentimental date, or a first-edition Elsie Dinsmore, or a tole pin tray, or a glass cherub

---

* Burlap or terry cloth make good ones. Line a big piece with plastic, fold it over, sew up the two sides, and run a drawstring through the end. Then appliqué a felt initial.

which might suit them exactly, and which they're not apt to run across, themselves.

Sick People in Hospital   Too many flowers can have the patient wondering uneasily if he's all that sick. Also, your pretty bouquet can be lost in the blooming confusion, so the patient can enjoy only the thought and not the flowers. It might be better to telephone the floor nurse before sending them, and ask how many other people beat you to it. If they didn't, this is one place where a corsage is good, for a woman, because it's *handleable,* and it brightens her hospital nightshirt.

And most people can use a packet of stamped post cards and a ball-point pen. Or a Thermos of orange juice spiked with vodka, if the patient misses his daily ration (and if it won't hurt him). Or a package of paperbacks, including an anthology of short pieces. Or a gift in several separately wrapped parts, each to be opened at a specified time. If your friend is especially fond of a particular country, a stereo viewer with slides is good. So is a big cake, if he's in a two-or-more-bed room. And gifts-to-get-well-for are encouraging: paid-up dinners, tickets, gift certificates.

But gifts of your own time can be better than anything. If your friend's room has a telephone, and this is an extended stay, it's a labor of love to copy his home telephone-index numbers into a dime-store telephone index for him, because the big phone book is awkward in bed. (You could bring the index from his house, of course, but his family may need it, too.) Or perhaps you could take dictation—written or typed—to help him catch up with his letters. And most women feel more cheerful with a fresh manicure. You might bring your own tools, or hers, and give her one.

The best hospital gift I ever received was Errands Done. When, with superb timing, I picked the week before Christmas to have a baby, a friend phoned me one morning. "I've a car and a free day," she said. "Give me your Christmas list!" It solved my problems, beautifully.

There is nothing like a gentle deed, so long as you don't do too many of them. It must be said that both good manners and good sense suggest that you stop doing them before they turn into uncomfortable obligations. In fact, if you feel too many gentle deeds coming on, you'd better stop and ask yourself why. As Nicholas Samstag has remarked, some people crowd their lives compulsively with these things "as if their only hope for happiness lay in winning some award as 'Best Friend of the Year.' " But most people would rather pedal their own bicycles for the most part, with only an occasional assist over a high curbstone.

Here, then, we'll consider some curbstones and ways to help people over them. It has been heartening to me, in my question-asking, to learn of the ways in which people have heartened each other.

First, a few general principles. It's usually unhelpful to say (as we all say, a thousand times in a lifetime), "Let me know if there's something I can do." Because—let's face it—he won't. Even if he should think of it, he won't. Either you think of it, or it won't get done.

And when you are thanked for doing a gentle deed, don't say, "Oh, it was no trouble—I was going there anyway," or "I've had that extra casserole in the freezer for weeks, anyway" or whatever it was. Because you're probably fibbing, at that, just to make the recipient feel less indebted. But if you're convincing enough, you've made it a case of the gift without the giver, and removed most of the warmth. It's better to say, "I'm so glad I was able to do it," or "It was a pleasure to do it for you"—either of which is probably more honest and also assures him he is liked or loved, as the case may be.

But back to that extra casserole, for food as a comforter is surely as old as trouble.

On moving day, friends of mine found a picnic hamper on their new front porch, full of beef sandwiches, potato chips, whole tomatoes, and milk for the kids.

I had had the flu for two weeks when a neighbor appeared one noon, with a purely marvelous lunch tray (just what she happened to have on hand, but it looked and tasted marvelous to me, who'd have settled for tea and an aspirin). I started to convalesce immediately.

The father of a friend of mine died. Before she left with her family for the funeral, her neighbor phoned, asked when they'd be back, and suggested they leave the door unlocked. Dinner was hot and ready in the oven when they returned.

People who can't cook, or don't, can bring food in time of trouble, too. They can arrange on a tray a rotisseried chicken or some sliced turkey, and some delicatessen coleslaw, with a loaf of fresh bread from a decent bakery, and a pile of grapes in the middle—then cover it with cellophane and leave it on the porch.

It's good to remember that, in times of grief, light food is often the best. A plate of small thin-sliced chicken sandwiches can be a most welcome offering.

Then, taking the children is a big thing. For an afternoon, for overnight, for a week or two, depending on the size of the trouble.

And chauffeuring is often a major help: doing the driving, parking, waiting, for all the small chores a friend needs to do the day before a big trip or a stay in the hospital.

So is staying with a friend the first day she's home from the hospital. (These days of shorter hospital stays, home is often a better place than the hospital to visit a sick friend, because while they're in the hospital, they're usually *sick*.)

The main thing is to think of a specific thing, then *do* it. And nearly always, your first thought is the thought to act on, for it comes from the intelligence of the heart.

There are many ways, indeed, to let people know you are standing by. One that I won't forget—it happens to be a combination of a gift and a gentle deed—was told to me by a friend of mine. She and her husband had had a warm, happy marriage; he died suddenly in September. Christmas was bleak for her, that year, but for the sake of her two young sons, she trimmed the traditional tree in their traditional way. Under the tree on Christmas morning she found a special gift for herself: a fifty-cent piece, wrapped as only a ten-year-old boy would wrap it, from Doug, the elder.

It had been his father's custom, you see, to give his mother, among her gifts, a small wrapped-up check. Now that Doug was the man of the family, he was doing the best he knew how to keep the old traditions alive.

CHAPTER FOURTEEN

Great Occasions: The Rites of Passage

"Rejoice with them that do rejoice, and weep with them that weep."
—ROMANS 12:15

It is curious that fair-weather friends—may their tribe increase —seem scarcer than the other kind. That is, for every person who rejoices with you when you find a pretty pebble, several would rather cry with you because you tripped on one. This is too bad, because in the strange mathematics of emotion, sharing someone's sorrow seldom cuts it in half, while sharing his joy can often double it.

Therefore, it is important that some people practice rejoicing—limbering up on the small good things that happen to people, and being glad about them, which will make rejoicing easier when it comes to the larger ones. Not only does this make living a little merrier for all concerned, it is part of the etiquette of great occasions: to add to another's joy, at a joyous time, quite as much as to assuage his grief at other sadder times, in whatever small ways one can.

This chapter will deal mainly, then, with the value of participating in great occasions, and only peripherally with their formalities, which are covered to the last tiring detail in the other etiquette books and don't matter much, anyway. (Few people actually *care* where the groom's family sits—on the right, on the left, in the middle—just so they're *there*, dressed up and acting nice.) Only a few small inflexibles will be found here, the doing or not doing of which could make one look foolish or unfeeling.

Now, it's true that in this mixed-up day of business-cum-social acquaintances, people are asked to rejoice in a tangible fashion more often than they should be, so that instead of feeling rejoiceful they feel railroaded.

Brides and brides' mothers often offend in this fashion without meaning to. Mrs. Bates, laboring under the delusion that her daughter's wedding and twelve-cylinder reception will pay off some social obligations, tends to send those thick creamy invitations to everyone she ever heard of.* But, of course, sacraments and social obligations really have nothing to do with each other.

And sometimes Mr. Bates gets into the spirit of the thing, too, adding the names of some people he does business with (who don't even know he has a daughter), and maybe the president of Outland Trust, just to keep things friendly.

But when you are on the receiving end of an invitation like this, it's hard to get into the spirit of the thing, yourself. While you're glad everything has worked out so nicely for the Bates girl, you can't exactly rejoice about it when you're not even

---

* She does all the minor things right: third person, hand addressing, dark blue or black ink, first-class mail, all that. It's her *list* that's wrong.

sure which one she is. About all you really feel is a regrettable suspicion that she's mighty anxious to complete her silver pattern.

It is time to state the rule clearly: Wedding invitations should be sent ONLY to people who have a reasonably warm, close relationship with at least one member of the families involved.

Now. As to what requires what:

A wedding announcement requires no reaction from you except kind thoughts. It is, after all, just a way of spreading the word. And Mrs. Bates should send announcements, not invitations, to people far away who wouldn't be able to come, though she may, of course, enclose a warm personal note if she likes.

A wedding invitation requires nothing, either (unless it says R.S.V.P., which they seldom do).

No reply.

No gift.

However, if you know the bride or the groom or the families, and are kindly disposed toward them so you can put your heart into it, it is a kindness to go and do them honor on this important occasion.

You never can tell, you see, how much space you occupy in someone else's life. It could be that you loom larger in theirs than vice versa. So, if you suspect this is the case but can't go, or don't feel up to it, it's good to write a warm note containing a legitimate-sounding excuse and your felicitations.

A wedding-and-reception invitation DOES require a reply—as the R.S.V.P. on the reception card indicates—but it does NOT necessarily require a gift.

It requires a reply because the bride's mother or the caterer will be concocting a lot of assorted goodies, and they must know how many people will be there to help eat and drink them up. And, in replying, you might as well follow the third-person format, because it's simpler than writing Mrs. Bates a cordial note. Also, it may be a bridal secretary, not Mrs. Bates or the bride-to-be, who'll be opening the returns. Telephoning Mrs. Bates would be an annoyance, and anyway, brides' mothers are practically impossible to catch.

As to the gift-or-not, this depends wholly on your genuine warm feelings about the whole thing. This is stressed, because there is a superstition abroad in our great land that a gift is the price of admission to the wedding reception. This is not so.

About Gifts   You may properly send a wedding gift at any time—before the wedding or after the wedding—but do not bring it to the scene of the ceremony.

Some people do, either because they were late getting it, or —perhaps—because they want to be sure they get full credit. I know an experienced bridal secretary who has philosophically accepted the fact that it will happen, and sees to it that one of the bride's friends stands ready at the church door with a roll of Scotch tape, to affix the donor's name securely to the gift, so the bride can thank her later. But it is an all-around nuisance.

As to sending a gift *after* the wedding: Some people would rather give something more imaginative than two dessert-spoons in the bride's preselected pattern. They prefer to wait till the couple is settled, so they can better select something personal or otherwise appropriate. This is perfectly correct, but it's best to explain the delay to the bride, or her feelings might be hurt.

Brides and Thank-yous   One of the inflexible rules is that brides MUST write thank-yous. If they don't, it embarrasses their mothers to death. Also, the people who sent the gifts won't ever know whether or not they arrived.

If the bride and groom are going on an extended honeymoon—say, a 'round-the-world tour—thank-you notes are sometimes postponed. I've seen small engraved cards sent out, under these circumstances, which said, "Your gift was received, and you will receive a note of appreciation in due course"—or something of the sort. This is pretty poor manners, if you ask me, though these people didn't. There's a certain feeling of the lackey waiting upon the Queen's nod here, which sits poorly with most people.

This little traveling bride could just as well have taken her list along with her and checked off three a day. The foreign stamps would provide an added touch. And she'd better not say, "Thank you so much for the lovely gift," either, because that's a dead giveaway that she doesn't know whether you supplied the pressed-glass pickle dish or the Jensen salad servers.

. . .

Unfortunately, we must mention, just in passing, the matter of bridal showers, which are usually as much fun as a case of sniffles, and, in the springtime, nearly as prevalent.

Now, a simple luncheon for the bride-to-be offers a good opportunity for communal rejoicing. But a shower too often provides the b-to-b with a bunch of mismated linens, and it gives the guests little cause for rejoicing, either, if they've been invited to too many (more than one is too many) for the same girl. At this rate, how can they hope to save anything up for their own hope chests?

It is superb good manners on the part of the prospective bride (should she sniff a few prospective showers to windward) to suggest to a good friend that these little groups merge on ONE shower—and preferably on one larger usable gift, too. If she hasn't shown this much perception, anyone giving a shower for her should ask each invitee if she has been already spoken for, and—if she has—promptly uninvite her.

The bride-to-be does NOT need to write thank-you notes to people whom she's already thanked in person at the shower. But she should write a note to her hostess. After all, her hostess went to a lot of trouble squiggling initials on all those *petits-fours*.

The Wedding Reception The big part of etiquette here is to let the guests exult and felicitate in reasonable comfort. The joy of the occasion decreases proportionately as the reception line lengthens.

"So nice . . . so lovely . . . so sweet . . ." people murmur, until they're out of adjectives and out of sorts, and there are still all those bridesmaids to go.

The bridal couple and both sets of parents are all that's necessary. *Bridesmaids* should not be in the reception line, for heaven's sake. Their job is to look pretty and circulate. The bride's mother—or hostess—should do the same thing, as soon as she reasonably can. Once most of the guests are assembled at the reception, she can—and should—play the part of a hostess: mingling, introducing, and so forth. I know a hostess who not only did so, but carried a campstool with her, to save herself fatigue and to bring herself down to the level of old ladies who were seated. She was a gracious lady and a fine hostess, and no one criticized a thing she did, either.

Food at wedding receptions should be reasonably neat to eat, for the guests are properly well bibbed and tuckered. Wedding cakes are untrustworthy, though, and in any case there should be plenty of napkins.

That's enough about weddings.

About Divorces These are not only a sad business, but a big nuisance, not only to the couple but to the couple's friends. When those pleasant people, the Bateses, stop being the Bateses, to everyone's astonishment, their mutual friends are often puzzled as to whether to go on seeing John, or Marcia, or both, and if so, how. (And the smaller the community, the untidier the situation can become.)

It's the part of good manners to make no judgments and take no sides here—after all, you'll never know exactly what Marcia did to John or John did to Marcia, no matter what either of them says—and it's the part of kindness to go on seeing them both, if you like them both. This you can do by entertaining them singly and alternately. They are both feeling bruised, and losing friends in addition to so much else is another bruise neither of them needs, no matter who was at fault.

John and Marcia can help things along, too, by not being unduly sensitive plants when they do happen, accidentally, to meet at a social gathering. After all, they stood each other for nine years, and they should be able to show reasonable courtesy for another couple of hours. (They needn't embrace with enthusiastic abandon as sometimes happens in some glossy circles. Just a tablespoonful of general good manners is all that's required.)

As to what Marcia will call herself from here on, modern manners give her plenty of leeway. If she wants to make her divorcée's status reasonably clear to everyone she may happen to meet, she can keep the Mrs., her maiden name, and her former husband's surname: "Mrs. Finnegan Bates." This is eminently proper. But maybe she never liked the name Finnegan. And certainly it could confuse friends and associates who may never have known that her maiden name was Finnegan. If she is a businesswoman, "Mrs. Marcia Bates" makes better practical sense, and it's a form you find more and more. (Indeed, it delivers the message that she is a divorcée quite as clearly as does "Mrs. Finnegan Bates," for had her husband died, she would still be Mrs. John Bates.)

Keeping the Bates is important, of course, because of the children. It's handier for mother and child to bear the same surname. If there are no children, though, and if Marcia doesn't like Bates's name any better than she likes Bates, she may correctly—with the aid of the court—go back to being Marcia Finnegan and take a fresh start.

WHEN SOMEONE IS GRADUATED

The etiquette of graduations depends largely on how important the occasion is in the life of the graduate.

Now, every life should have some ceremony in it; and these ceremonies should be honored by the friends of the person who's living this particular life.

If the graduate is being graduated from high school—with no intentions of going on to college or to a university—it is correspondingly more important to him. Therefore, should you be so unlucky as to receive an invitation to his high-school Commencement, you must *go,* even though there are few duller ways to spend a soft spring evening. But you must go anyway, applauding in the right places and congratulating your friend later, in person. For this, to him, is a Great Occasion.

Good manners also require that you send the graduate a gift (to arrive, preferably, before the ceremony). Good stationery is a good choice, for college graduates, too. If you are sure of the graduate's taste, you can have engraved writing paper made, or a monogram carved (or whatever it is these places do) so he can replenish his stationery supplies later on. He can use this writing paper in applying for a job, perhaps, and in thanking you for the writing paper.

However, if the high-school graduate is going on to college, you can save your fire for another four years. For in this case, the high-school graduate probably doesn't think it's too important, either. You can send him a small gift and a congratulatory note; and you can get out of going to the Commencement exercises with a good Social Lie.

Just make sure it *is* a good one, and that you deliver it early enough so he can send that little invitation card (they're allowed a limited number, usually) to someone else and thus get another present.

ON BECOMING A VITAL STATISTIC

All of us do, at least twice: once when we are born, and again when we die. And it's curious that we can't do a thing for ourselves at either of these two times—surely the two most important moments in anyone's life. We must depend on other people to do what needs doing, and they must depend on us. The etiquette of these occasions is correspondingly important.

WHEN SOMEONE DIES

We must differentiate here between the good friend who dies (or relative of a good friend) and the good acquaintance, whose death you read about in the newspaper.

In the latter case, it is important to follow whatever suggestions are given in the obituary notice, even though you might, personally, prefer to do something else. If there is a mention of memorial contributions*—to a medical research or other special fund—and you would rather pay to have yearly Masses said for the dead person, it would be poor to do so. This fund was probably dear to his heart, or it is dear to the heart of the family, and he would be pretty miffed if he knew what you had done (and the family probably *will* be miffed). If the notice says "Please omit flowers," then omit them, by all means. There may be emotional reasons. Or religious ones: Orthodox Jewish funerals do not permit flowers, nor are they desired at Reform or Conservative Jewish funerals. Nor is it good to send them directly to a Catholic church where—usually—only the family's one spray of flowers is permitted, in addition to the altar arrangement.

If no mention is made of a memorial contribution or of flowers, and you would still like to make known your concern, it is good to send flowers to the survivor most closely involved, a few days after the services. A note—"My thoughts are with you," or "With deep affection"—will indicate your feelings.

When there are no special directions given in the obituary

---

* The news that you contributed will be received by the family of the person who died, although the amount that you give will not ordinarily be specified.

notice, you may, of course, send flowers to the funeral chapel (or wherever the services will be held, with the exceptions mentioned above). You do not address them to Edward Brown —if Edward Brown is the person who died—but to the funeral of Edward Brown. This, by the way, is one of the inflexibles.

And, of course, to Edward's widow—or whoever is most immediately concerned—a note can be quite as comforting as flowers, and is often more so. And let it be said in large type, A NOTE IS ALWAYS BETTER THAN A TELEPHONE CALL, IN TIMES OF GRIEF.

Of course, notes present a problem: what to say. One wants to make one's sorrow known, without increasing someone else's. The simplest thing is always the best: "We heard the news with a real sense of loss. Edward meant so much to the whole community, and we will miss him."

If Edward's path has crossed your own in some way, it is heartening, not saddening, to mention it. "I won't forget Edward's kindness to me, when . . ." and then what happened.

Or, if Edward hadn't the opportunity to be kind to you, personally, but you knew him to be a generally valuable person, "Just knowing someone like Edward has been an important thing in my life, and I can deeply appreciate the magnitude of your loss. . . ." It is a simple thing, and a helpful one, to express what you feel in times of sorrow.

It is also good to write "Please don't bother to answer this" at the bottom of your note. Many people will answer it anyway, for doing these small jobs can be therapeutic in helping to pull the sorrowing person back to solid ground. On the other hand, he won't feel obligated, if answering letters at this time is the last thing he feels up to doing.

As for the etiquette rules about thanking the flower donors— people should thank them, just as any gift properly requires thanks. But if the friends are worth having, they'll think nothing of it if they *don't*.

Whoever receives the flowers may write, "Your kind expression of sympathy was greatly appreciated, and the white roses comforted me," or something of this sort. But so far as I'm concerned, he doesn't need to. Grief is grief; he needn't pamper my small feelings, unless it helps him to do so, when he is wholly engaged in the larger battles of the soul. And there's no point whatsoever in his sending those sterile printed thank-you forms.

When a good friend dies—or the close relative of a good friend—it's not mainly a matter of what the obituary notice tells you to do (though, of course, you observe this), but what your own heart tells you to do. Usually, one should follow his first impulse, for it is usually the right one. What could you do wrong, if you are a well-meaning person? Even though the thing you do has been done, or didn't need doing, your being there is what counts and comforts.

Some people—and this is where the intelligence of the heart enters—need to be left alone, to work things out for themselves. Then it is good to leave a letter in the mailbox saying that you understand this but are standing by.

Other people need someone with them. But you know this, knowing your friends; if you're in a position to do so, you can offer your own guest room, or possibly arrange to stay with him.

In any case, things need to be done. Volunteering to telephone friends and acquaintances can be helpful. Or preparing the obituary notice for the newspapers. Or taking the children for a while. Or taking care of any essential correspondence. Or boarding the pets.

Bringing food is a traditional comforting gesture in time of grief. Don't worry lest other people may have done so, too. The food can be eaten, or frozen, and at any rate you did what you thought of doing.

A thoughtful thing for a good friend to do, in most circumstances, is to arrange a get-together of a few friends, for food and drink, after the services. This, like the old-fashioned wake, can be of great help; for an empty house is a bleak house after a funeral. The affair is usually emotional, with reminiscences —both sad and merry—of the person who has died. But it is a cathartic, constructive emotion that helps to guide the sorrowing people from the country of grief back into the land of the living.

Taps, at a military funeral, is followed by a brisk march.

HONORABLE BABY

A big thing to remember is that every new baby deserves homage, even one to whom you haven't been introduced. When you see a tiny new baby and its mother, it is only courteous to give it a warm, kind look, for, to its mother, it is probably quite a special baby, with its square feet and everything.

Now, a baby announcement requires no reply, although it's good to send a card—"Hooray for John Wesley, Jr!" or whatever you like—to indicate that you're cheering.

It is a big etiquette boner for a relative to give a baby shower. Only friends can do this. Also, baby showers are only for *first* babies. One baby shower is enough.

For christening, see any other etiquette book; customs differ greatly according to religions and locales. One point that's nearly standard, however, is to slip the officiating clergyman $10 or more in a plain envelope when the proceedings are over.

In giving a baby gift, it is a good idea to give one with some staying power, especially if you're closely related—by friendship or family—to this particular baby. Of course, there are other things than silver porringers and cups, although those are very nice. There are also silver diaper pins. Even gold diaper pins. And there are candles measured to burn an inch for 21 birthdays. Or a bank account opened with $5 or more, earmarked to help with his first bicycle or trip to Disneyland. Then there is the old custom—and a pretty custom it is—of giving a bottle of good wine (ask your friendly neighborhood wine merchant which kind won't deteriorate) to be laid on its side in a cool dark place and opened on his 21st birthday.

And there it is—for a book, like a dinner party or a wedding or a christening or a life, must sometime come to an end. Then one wonders what to say. What should be the final word or the moral, if there be one?

Well, perhaps it can be this: The heart of the etiquette that matters is to rejoice with them that do rejoice, and to weep with them that weep, remembering, and trying to help them remember, that for every door that closes another opens.

> *"How pleasant is Saturday night,*
> *When I've tried all the week to be good,*
> *Not spoken a word that was bad,*
> *And obliged everyone that I could."*
>
> —ANONYMOUS
> Capper's Weekly, CIRCA 1911

Index